THE
APPROACHING
APOCALYPSE

What You Should Know About
The End Time and
The Return of Christ

ROBERT I. ADAMS

Copyright © 2012-2018 Robert I. Adams

First printing: 2012
Second Expanded Edition: 2015
Third Expanded Edition: 2016
Fourth Expanded Edition: 2018

All rights reserved. This book or any portion thereof may not be reproduced or used in any manner whatsoever without the express written permission of the publisher except for the use of brief quotations in a book review or scholarly journal.

Maps by Robert I. Adams

ISBN 978-1-105-97318-5

Lulu Publishing Services

Scripture quotations are primarily from New King James Version and New International Version. Other translations used include The Amplified Bible (AMP), American Standard Version (ASV), King James Version (KJV), and New American Standard Bible (NASB).

All italics and words in brackets within Scripture quotations are the author's with the exception of quotes from The Amplified Bible.

About the title: The word 'apocalypse' is derived from the Greek word *apokalupsis*, which means 'appearing,' 'coming,' 'manifestation,' 'revelation.'

More copies can be ordered from Lulu.com (write the title in the search box).

Comments and questions are welcome, and can be sent to the author: roivad@sf-nett.no

Author's website: www.lastdaysdetective.com

Contents

Introduction

SECTION 1   THE GREAT TRIAL

Part 1   *A Time of Tribulation*

Chapter 1	What Is It All About?	13
Chapter 2	When Will It Begin?	18
Chapter 3	How Long Will It Last?	22

Part 2   *Before the Tribulation*

Chapter 4	End Time Horsemen	27
Chapter 5	The Eleventh King	31
Chapter 6	The Growing Horn	35
Chapter 7	The Treaty and the Temple	41

Part 3   *During the Tribulation*

Chapter 8	The Kingdom of the Beast	49
Chapter 9	The Decree of the False Prophet	55
Chapter 10	Saints in the Tribulation	60
Chapter 11	The Woman and the Witnesses	65
Chapter 12	Death and Destruction	70

Part 4	*After the Tribulation*	
Chapter 13	The Revelation of the Redeemer	77
Chapter 14	The Great Gathering	80
Chapter 15	Christ versus Antichrist	85
Chapter 16	The Coming Kingdom	89

Part 5	*The Time is Drawing Near*	
Chapter 17	In Preparation	97
Chapter 18	Overcoming in the Last Days	101
Chapter 19	Staying Awake	106

SECTION 2 WHAT ABOUT THE RAPTURE?

Part 6	*Theory and Reality*	
Chapter 20	A Question of Timing	115
Chapter 21	Prophetic Scriptures and the End Time	121
Chapter 22	Theories about the Return of Christ	126

Part 7	*Under the Magnifying Glass*	
Chapter 23	Can Christ Return at Any Moment?	135
Chapter 24	Will the Church Avoid the Tribulation?	139
Chapter 25	Will Christ Fetch the Church to Heaven?	143

| Chapter 26 | God's Wrath and the Heavenly Elders | 148 |
| Chapter 27 | Will the Church See the Antichrist? | 156 |

Part 8 *The Last Stones Unturned*

Answering More Arguments	165
From the Old Testament	166
From the Gospels	175
From the Letters	200
From the Book of Revelation	219

A Final Word	245
About the Author	246
Bibliography	247

Introduction

The pace in today's world is getting quicker. Things change fast and what was considered unlikely a few years ago, is now reality. In step with these changes, we are moving toward a state of affairs the Bible prophesies about. According to Scripture, a short and intense period is coming the world has never witnessed before. It will be a time of massive seduction, unspeakable evil, and enormous destruction. People everywhere will have to choose whom they will give their allegiance to—either the ruler of this world or the Lord Jesus.

Those who believe in Jesus will risk being persecuted to death. War will cause horrific casualties. The world will come to the edge of the precipice. Only an act of God can save humanity from complete annihilation—He is going to send His Son back to the earth with power and great glory. The second coming of Christ will bring to an end man's failed attempt to govern the earth. As supreme monarch, Jesus will reign with perfect righteousness in a new world together with those who love Him.

The Bible gives us many details about what will happen in the end time. Let's explore the prophetic landscape and map out the prospects. Soon the time will arrive, so we cannot afford to be uninformed about the coming great drama.

In the first half of this book, I show from Scripture what is going to take place before Jesus comes, when He comes, and after He comes. In addition, I address the issue of preparation. The second half deals with the rapture—the catching up of the saints to meet Jesus. I leave no stone unturned in presenting what the Bible really says about it, and when it will occur in relation to end time events.

It is my desire that what you read will cause you to say from your heart, "Even so, come, Lord Jesus" (Rev. 22:20).

SECTION 1

THE GREAT TRIAL

Part 1

A Time of Tribulation

Chapter 1

What Is It All About?

Prophetic statements in the Bible are amazing. Many of them concern the first coming of Christ, uttered centuries beforehand. Other prophecies foretell the course of history, cross our time and reach into the future. Still others concentrate on a confined period leading up to the second coming of Christ.

The last book of the Bible tells of "the hour of trial that is going to come upon the whole world to test those who live on the earth" (Rev. 3:10). This coming time will involve "every nation, tribe, people and language" (Rev. 7:9), and is called "the great tribulation" (Rev. 7:14).

The term *tribulation* originally meant 'pressure' in the Greek language of the New Testament. It was used to describe the pressure of circumstances, especially during persecution. Jesus referred to this when He spoke to His disciples about the future. He said:

> They will deliver you up to tribulation and kill you, and you will be hated by all nations for My name's sake. (Matt. 24:9)

Later on in the same discourse, Jesus mentioned the coming period of great tribulation:

> Then there will be great tribulation, such as has not been since the beginning of the world until this time, no, nor ever shall be. (Matt. 24:21)

Jesus then said, "Immediately after the tribulation of those days" (Matt. 24:29) He will seen "coming on the clouds of the sky, with power and great glory" (Matt. 24:30).

Summary: Just before Jesus comes back in glory, there will be a time of unprecedented pressure and persecution on a global scale.

BIRTH PAINS

In His end time discourse, Jesus mentioned the coming of false messiahs, as well as wars, famines, and earthquakes (Matt. 24:5–7). Then He said, "All these are the *beginning* of birth pains" (Matt. 24:8). This shows us that when Jesus went on to talk about the great tribulation (v.21), He is comparing this period to a woman's *last* rigorous birth pains. There will be widespread religious seduction, escalating conflict, severe catastrophes, and massive destruction across the globe. Jesus explained that these "birth pains" would happen just prior to His return, which He spoke of later in the chapter:

> Immediately after the tribulation of those days the sun will be darkened, and the moon will not give its light; the stars will fall from heaven, and the powers of the heavens will be shaken. Then the sign of the Son of Man will appear in heaven, and then all the tribes of the earth will mourn, and they will see the Son of Man coming on the clouds of heaven with power and great glory. (Matt. 24:29, 30)

The return of Christ will mark the beginning of a new age, which Jesus called "the age to come" (Mark 10:30). He called the future transition from the present age, "the regeneration" (Matt. 19:28). The rebirth of the world will come after the great tribulation—the time of the last "birth pains."

Summary: In the great tribulation just before Jesus comes back in glory there will be widespread religious seduction, as well as world conflict, immense catastrophes, and huge earthquakes causing much destruction across the entire globe.

JUDGMENTS OF GOD

The great tribulation will be a time full of divine acts of judgment. God is going to judge evil on the earth. When ungodliness has fully ripened, then judgment will come.

It is my opinion the main part of the book of Revelation describes God's judgments in the coming tribulation period. He will allow plagues to wreak havoc. Among the things that are going to happen will be fires that destroy vast areas, contamination that causes the death of numerous sea creatures, the destruction of many ships by huge tsunamis, and fresh water sources that become poisonous (cf. Rev. 8:7–11).

Through everything that is going to happen, God will call people to repentance and salvation before it is too late. Even so, many people will refuse to repent of their sin:

> The rest of mankind that were not killed by these plagues still did not repent of the work of their hands; they did not stop worshiping demons, and idols. . . . Nor did they repent of their murders, their magic arts, their sexual immorality or their thefts. (Rev. 9:20, 21)

The chastising judgments of God will come in the course of the great tribulation. As for the wrath of God, it will be poured out upon sinners, but apparently not before the very end of the great tribulation (cf. Rev. 16:1 ff). God's wrath will come in different forms—such as loathsome sores, intense heat from the sun, pitch darkness in the day time, and a massive worldwide earthquake that destroys whole cities.

Summary: During the great tribulation, God is going to judge evil on the earth with various plagues. This will culminate with God's wrath being manifested.

JEWS AND JESUS

Besides being a time of divine judgment, the great tribulation is also going to be a time when the Lord will confront the people of Israel. He is going to awaken the Jews so they will acknowledge their apostasy. God's aim will be to bring them back into a right relationship to their King. In the course of the tribulation period, the Jews will be prepared to receive their Messiah when He returns in glory.

The Lord said the following about His ascension and about the Jews in the end time:

> I will return to My place [on high] until they acknowledge their offence and feel their guilt and seek My face; in their affliction and distress they will seek, inquire for, and require Me earnestly. (Hos. 5:15 AMP)

According to the prophet Zechariah, the Jews will be put to the test and will at last call on the name of the Lord (cf. Zech. 13:9). The great tribulation will urge the Jewish nation to plead God to send the Messiah. When the Jews have gone through the very difficult time ahead, they will at last cry out, "Blessed is he who comes in the name of the Lord" (Matt. 23:39).

The Lord has promised:

> And I will pour out on the house of David and the inhabitants of Jerusalem a spirit of grace and supplication. They will look on me, the one they have pierced. (Zech. 12:10)

When the surviving Jews experience this at the return of Christ, the result will be national regeneration: "And so all Israel will be saved" (Rom. 11:26).

Summary: God is going to use the great tribulation to cause Jews who survive this time to call on the Lord Jesus and receive Him when He returns.

THE FAITHFUL

The great tribulation will be a time of severe anguish for those who believe in Jesus Christ. They will be systematically ousted and oppressed by Satan's minions. In the book of Revelation they are described as those who "have the testimony of Jesus Christ" (Rev. 12:17), and who "obey God's commandments and remain faithful to Jesus" (Rev. 14:12). We are told of their tears (Rev. 7:17), their prayers (Rev. 8:3), their testimony (Rev. 12:11), their patience and faith (Rev. 13:10), their labors (Rev. 14:13), as well as their spilt blood (Rev. 16:6; 17:6; 18:24; 19:2).

In the tribulation period, believers will be refined and prepared to meet the Lord when He returns to the earth. Daniel 11:35 says, "And some of those of understanding shall fall [by sword and flame – v.33], to refine them, purify them, and make them white, until the time of the end." Revelation 20:4 says those who will be executed in the great tribulation "for their witness to Jesus" are going to reign with Him in His coming kingdom.

Summary: The trials of the great tribulation are going to refine those who believe in Jesus Christ and prepare them for His return.

Chapter 2

When Will It Begin?

Now that we are aware of what the great tribulation is all about, we need to find out whether it is possible to know when it will happen. The Bible does not provide us with a date, but it does present an incident that marks the starting point of the great tribulation. Jesus informs us about this in His end time discourse:

> So when you see *standing in the holy place the abomination that causes desolation, spoken of through the prophet Daniel*—let the reader understand—then let those who are in Judea flee to the mountains. . . . For *then there will be great tribulation*, such as has not been since the beginning of the world until this time, no, nor ever shall be. (Matt. 24:15, 16, 21)

From this, we understand that when "the abomination that causes desolation" stands in "the holy place" then the great tribulation will begin. We have, therefore, to find out where "the holy place" is, and what "the abomination that causes desolation" is.

According to Jesus, this fateful event was "spoken of through the prophet Daniel" (Matt. 24:15). Turning to the book of Daniel, we find what Jesus referred to in chapter 11:

> His armed forces will rise up to desecrate the temple fortress

and will abolish the daily sacrifice. Then they will set up *the abomination that causes desolation*. (Dan. 11:31)

This verse tells us "the abomination that causes desolation" will be set up in "the temple fortress." This must be the site of "the holy place," where Jesus says "the abomination that causes desolation" will stand.

THE TEMPLE OF GOD

"The holy place" and "the temple fortress" definitely point to a Jewish temple in Jerusalem. The fact that Jesus mentions Judea in the prophecy (cf. Matt. 24:16) supports this assertion, since Jerusalem is situated in that area.

Seeing this is a prophecy of the end time, it must necessarily presuppose that a new Jewish temple will be constructed in Jerusalem. This assumption is substantiated by the presence of Jewish groups, who with increasing intensity are now preparing for the rebuilding of the temple. Suffice to say, both Paul and John wrote of a physical structure in the end time called "the temple of God" (2 Thess. 2:4; Rev. 11:1). In a later chapter, we shall take a closer look at the temple prophecies and the preparations for its rebuilding.

Looking again at Daniel's prophecy, we see what will happen to the temple: "Armed forces will rise up to desecrate the temple fortress and will abolish the daily sacrifice" (Dan. 11:31). What "the daily sacrifice" here entails is described in Numbers 28:3–8, where a prescribed offering is presented to the Lord as "a regular burnt offering each day." Having in mind that Daniel's prophecy is going to be fulfilled in the end time, we must conclude that the ancient system of offerings will be restored when a new temple is built.

THE MAN OF SIN

Let's now move on to identify "the abomination that causes desolation" mentioned by the prophet Daniel and referred to by Christ. In Mark's version of Christ's end time discourse, we see that it involves a certain man:

> But when ye see the abomination of desolation standing where *he* ought not (let him that readeth understand), then let them that are in Judea flee unto the mountains. (Mark 13:14 ASV)

This person seems to be the one Paul wrote about:

> Let no one deceive you by any means; for that Day will not come unless the falling away comes first, and *the man of sin* is revealed, *the son of perdition*, who opposes and exalts himself above all that is called God or that is worshiped, so that *he sits as God in the temple of God*, showing himself that he is God. (2 Thess. 2:3, 4)

Here we see how "the man of sin" sets himself up in the temple of God, i.e. the end time temple in Jerusalem. This explains what Jesus said in Mark 13:14 concerning the one who will be "standing where he ought not." The man referred to here is undeniably the one who is mentioned in Daniel 11:31:

> *His* armed forces will rise up to desecrate the temple fortress and will abolish the daily sacrifice. Then they will set up the abomination that causes desolation.

From what is written earlier in Daniel 11, we understand that this man is one of the "kings" (v.27) in this chapter. He is also present in chapter 9:

> *He* will . . . put an end to sacrifice and offering. And at the temple *he* will set up an abomination that causes desolation. (Dan. 9:27)

The man who is spoken of here will "put an end to sacrifice and offering." In other words, he will "abolish the daily sacrifice"

(Dan. 11:31). Then he will set up "an abomination that causes desolation."

THE FINAL ABOMINATION

What then is "the abomination that causes desolation," which according to the prophecy will stand in a future temple in Jerusalem?

The word "abomination" in the Hebrew text is, among other things, used of idols that desecrated the temple of the Lord. The prophet Jeremiah wrote:

> For the children of Judah have done evil in My sight, says the Lord. They have set their *abominations* in the house which is called by My name, to pollute it. (Jer. 7:30)

From what we have seen, the final idolatrous abomination in God's house will be "the man of sin" setting himself up in a future temple in Jerusalem and proclaiming himself to be God. This abomination will then cause desolation in Jerusalem and further abroad.

The one who will perpetrate the coming "abomination that causes desolation" is the one who the apostle John warned of when he wrote, "You have heard that the Antichrist is coming" (1 John 2:18). This man will enter the rebuilt temple and make his blasphemous declaration. According to Jesus, this event will mark the beginning of the great tribulation.

Chapter 3

How Long Will It Last?

We need not be ignorant about the length of the great tribulation because the Bible doesn't leave us in the dark. To arrive at the answer, let's take another look at a verse we stopped by in the last chapter:

> His armed forces will rise up to desecrate the temple fortress and will abolish the daily sacrifice. Then they will set up the abomination that causes desolation. (Dan. 11:31)

We found out Jesus says this will be the starting point of the great tribulation. In the next chapter in the book of Daniel, we read about a number of days after the events that mark the beginning of the great tribulation: "From the time that the daily sacrifice is abolished and the abomination that causes desolation is set up, there will be 1,290 days" (Dan. 12:11). The period of 1,290 days is equivalent to three and a half years. We can compare this to what we find earlier in the same chapter:

> There will be *a time of distress* such as has not happened from the beginning of nations until then. . . .
> Then I, Daniel, looked, and there before me stood two others. . . . One of them said to the man clothed in linen, who was above the waters of the river, *'How long will it be before these astonishing things are fulfilled?'* The man clothed in linen, who was above the waters of the river, lifted his right and his left hand toward heaven, and I heard him swear by

Him who lives forever, saying, *'It will be for a time, times and half a time.'* (Dan. 12:1, 5–7)

We see here the "time of distress," i.e. the great tribulation, is going to last "a time, times and half a time." This period in the book of Daniel is also mentioned in the book of Revelation:

The woman was given the two wings of a great eagle, so that she might fly to the place prepared for her in the desert, where she would be taken care of for *a time, times and half a time*, out of the serpent's reach. (Rev. 12:14)

The expression "a time, times and half a time" is also portrayed another way in the same chapter:

The woman fled into the desert to a place prepared for her by God, where she might be taken care of for *1,260 days*. (Rev. 12:6)

The same amount of days is also found in the preceding chapter:

And I will give power to my two witnesses, and they will prophesy for *1,260 days*, clothed in sackcloth. (Rev. 11:3)

The period of 1,260 days is equivalent to three and a half years. This time is also rendered in months in two other references:

The beast was given a mouth to utter proud words and blasphemies and to exercise his authority for *forty-two months*. (Rev. 13:5)

The Gentiles . . . will trample on the holy city for *forty-two months*. (Rev. 11:2)

The prophecies imply that the timeframe of the great tribulation is three and a half years. Obviously, the forty-two months or 1,260 days fall within the 1,290 days previously mentioned. That this amounts to a literal period of three and a half years should be evident. A comparison can be made to Christ's words concerning Elijah's time when "the sky was shut for three and a half years" (Luke 4:25).

IN THE MIDDLE OF THE SEVEN

Some expositors have the notion that the great tribulation will last seven years. This idea is based on Daniel 9:27, which mentions a period of "seven" in the end time. The meaning of this "seven" is apparently seven years. The great tribulation is certainly connected to this period, but will not last the whole of it because of what is written in the same verse:

> In the middle of the 'seven' he will put an end to sacrifice and offering. And at the temple he will set up an abomination that causes desolation. (Dan. 9:27)

We have already seen that what happens in the middle of the 'seven' triggers the great tribulation. From then on only half of the 'seven' remains, which represents three and a half years. It is during this short time the great tribulation will run its course.

One of the reasons why the great tribulation will be short can been seen from what Christ says about this time:

> If those days had not been cut short, no one would survive, but for the sake of the elect those days will be shortened. (Matt. 24:22)

From the continuation of Christ's end time discourse, the great tribulation will come to an abrupt end when He is revealed from heaven at His return (cf. Matt. 24:29, 30).

Part 2

Before the Tribulation

Chapter 4

End Time Horsemen

When Jesus spoke of the end time, He not only prophesied about the great tribulation, but also about several things that will occur before this period. He talked about these things in Matthew 24.

Now if we compare what Jesus says in Matthew 24 to prophetic events the apostle John describes in Revelation 6, we can see points of resemblance. In Revelation 6, a series of events take place as Jesus opens seals on a scroll in heaven. It is apparent that His end time discourse in Matthew 24 sheds light on the meaning of the scenes John saw. The following is a comparison of what the opening of the first four seals entails and what Jesus predicted:

> *John*: Now I saw when the Lamb [Christ] opened one of the seals; and I heard one of the four living creatures saying with a voice like thunder, 'Come and see.' And I looked, and behold, a white horse. He who sat on it had a bow; and a crown was given to him, and he went out conquering and to conquer. (Rev. 6:1, 2)

> *Jesus*: For many will come in My name, saying, 'I am the Christ,' and will deceive many. (Matt. 24:5)

The rider on the white horse seems to reflect seductive imitations of Jesus Christ, who also rides a white horse (Rev.

19:11). By deceit, they succeed in leading astray and capturing people's hearts. More false christs have appeared in the last generation than in any other generation since the birth of Christ.

In its final form, the rider is an illustration of the end time Antichrist. He will be the most prominent of all false messiahs who will "deceive many" (Matt. 24:5). Even his title suggests this; 'Anti' implies being 'instead of,' as well as 'against,' and 'christ' means 'messiah.'

The Antichrist will be a false savior "proclaiming himself to be God" (2 Thess. 2:4). His coming will be "according to the working of Satan, with all power, signs, and lying wonders" (2 Thess. 2:9). These things also mark the false messiahs who Jesus said, "will appear and perform great signs and miracles" (Matt. 24:24).

The bow the rider carries can be regarded as symbolic of Satan's weaponry. In Ephesians 6:16, the believers are told to take up the shield of faith, with which they can "extinguish all the flaming arrows of the evil one." These arrows are shot from his bow. We must therefore keep a look out. Jesus warned, "Watch out that no one deceives you" (Matt. 24:4).

WARS—FAMINES—PESTILENCE

We will now look at the second, third, and fourth seals and their explanation:

> *John*: When the Lamb opened the second seal, I heard the second living creature say, 'Come!' Then another horse came out, a fiery red one. Its rider was given power to take peace from the earth and to make men slay each other. To him was given a large sword. (Rev. 6:3, 4)

> *Jesus*: You will hear of wars and rumors of wars, but see to it that you are not alarmed. Such things must happen, but the end is still to come. Nation will rise against nation, and kingdom against kingdom. (Matt. 24:6, 7a)

The twentieth century witnessed two world wars and many

other wars in different parts of the globe. Studies have shown that the amount of deaths caused by war in the twentieth century was more than thirty times higher than in the previous one. During the last half century alone there have been more than one hundred different wars, including civil wars. Jesus said, "Such things must happen, but the end is still to come" (Matt. 24:6).

> *John*: When the Lamb opened the third seal, I heard the third living creature say, 'Come!' I looked, and there before me was a black horse! Its rider was holding a pair of scales in his hand. Then I heard what sounded like a voice among the four living creatures, saying, 'A quart of wheat for a day's wages, and three quarts of barley for a day's wages.' (Rev. 6:5, 6)

Jesus: There will be famines. (Matt. 24:7b)

A comparison to conditions at the time of the apostle John shows the price of food rises 800 percent. Such a hyperinflation would follow in the wake of a paralyzing famine.

The last century witnessed large famines in Russia (1921, 1947), China (1928-30, 1936, 1942-43, 1959-61), Ethiopia (1958, 1972-73, 1984-85), and North Korea (1996). Untold millions died.

> *John*: When the Lamb opened the fourth seal, I heard the voice of the fourth living creature say, 'Come!' I looked, and there before me was a pale horse! Its rider was named Death, and Hades was following close behind him. (Rev. 6:7, 8)

Jesus: . . . and pestilences. (Matt. 24:7c KJV)

Pestilence has many faces, e.g.: HIV, AIDS, tuberculosis, cancer, malaria, parasites, pneumonia, and various infectious diseases. Many plagues, epidemics, and pandemics have ravaged the world the last century, killing millions of people.

THE BEGINNING OF BIRTH PAINS

The things we have looked at from Matthew 24 that Jesus spoke of are in verses 5, 6, and 7, while the great tribulation is described from verse 21 onward. It is therefore obvious that the first four things Jesus tells about occur *before* the great tribulation.

As we have already noted, Jesus says in verse 8, "All these are the beginning of birth pains." In other words, Jesus likened the things he talked about to birth pains showing that a birth will occur soon. Birth pains are intense and when they come with increasingly shorter intervals, they get worse until the delivery is completed. That is the way it will be in the world in the end time. There will be more and more false messiahs who will deceive many. Wars, famines, and pestilence will increase in number and intensity as the great tribulation and the second coming of Christ draw closer.

The horsemen in Revelation 6 cause a horror that has a collective effect. The first horseman is not replaced by the second, etc. Instead, the first horseman (false messiahs, and finally the Antichrist) is accompanied by the second (war), the third (famine), and the fourth (pestilence). The combined effect of the four horsemen is catastrophic. They will have lethal power over a considerable part of the world:

> They were given power over a fourth of the earth to kill by sword [the fiery red horse], famine [the black horse] and plague [the pale horse], and by the wild beasts of the earth. (Rev. 6:8)

This belongs to the future, but already now, we can hear the hoof beats of the end time horses.

Chapter 5

The Eleventh King

Six hundred years before the time of Christ, the prophet Daniel received visions concerning the future. He saw kingdoms in the form of wild beasts, and previewed the end time. Daniel prophesied about the Babylonian Empire, the Medo-Persian Empire, the Grecian Empire, and yet another empire:

> Daniel said, 'I was looking in my vision by night, and behold, the four winds of heaven were stirring up the great sea. And four great beasts were coming up from the sea, different from one another. The first was like a lion and had the wings of an eagle. . . . And behold, another beast, a second one, resembling a bear. . . . After this I kept looking, and behold, another one, like a leopard which had on its back four wings of a bird; the beast had also four heads, and dominion was given to it. After this I kept looking in the night visions, and behold, a fourth beast, dreadful and terrifying and extremely strong; and it had large iron teeth. It devoured and crushed and trampled down the remainder with its feet; and it was different from all the beasts that were before it, and it had ten horns.' (Dan. 7:2–7)

The fourth beast that Daniel saw in his night vision symbolized the Roman Empire, which militarily was "terrifying and frightening and very powerful." At its greatest extent, the empire was comprised of the landmass around the Mediterranean Sea, from Portugal in the west to Iraq in the east.

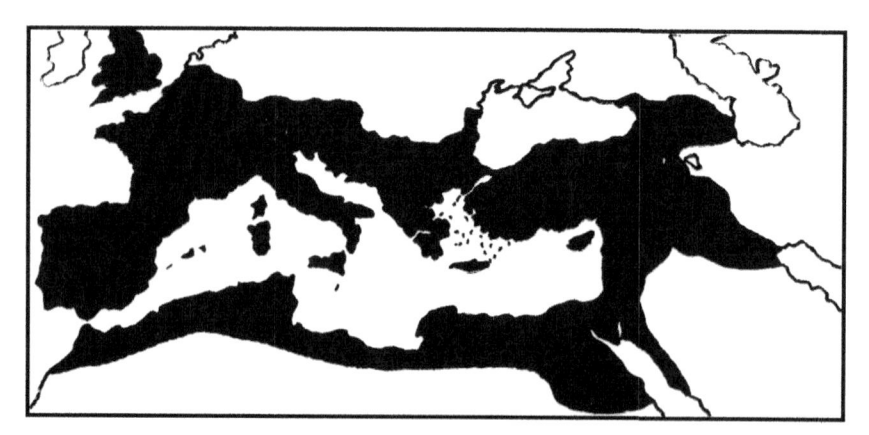

The Roman Empire

TEN KINGS AND ANOTHER KING

Daniel noticed that the beast had ten horns. An angel explained to Daniel what they meant: "The ten horns are ten kings who will come from this kingdom" (Dan. 7:24). This presupposed that the Roman Empire would be broken up. In the fourth century A.D., the empire was divided between east and west. Then in the fifth century, various people groups divided the Western Roman Empire between themselves. The Eastern Roman Empire lasted one thousand years longer before being conquered by the Ottoman (Islamic) Empire. The division of this area into the countries of today began as late as after the First World War.

The "ten kings" who Daniel prophesied about appear to be a coalition of ten leaders who will arise from within the area of the ancient Roman Empire. In the process toward this state of affairs, many have looked to The European Union, especially in its early days. Yet today, the EU consists of more than twenty-five countries, and some of them are not situated within the landmass of the ancient Roman Empire. Due to the amount of member countries and their geographical location, the EU is obviously not what was prophesied about.

Some suggest the ten "kings" in Daniel's prophecy arise in Western Europe as part of the EU, but it is quite plausible the prophecy points to the eastern part of the ancient Roman Empire. This area is predominately Muslim. Fourteen Muslim countries are situated wholly or partially within what was the landmass of the Roman Empire (more on this in the next chapter).

Look now at what happens in the continuation of Daniel's vision: "While I was thinking about the [ten] horns, there before me was another horn, a little one, which came up among them; and three of the first horns were uprooted before it" (Dan. 7:8). Here follows the explanation the angel gave to Daniel: "After them [the ten kings] another king will arise, different from the earlier ones; he will subdue three kings" (Dan. 7:24). In other words, from among a coalition of ten rulers who exercise authority within the borders of the ancient Roman Empire a new ruler will arise who will suppress three of them.

We are told the new horn "looked more imposing than the others" (Dan. 7:20). The horn that begins as "a little one" grows until it becomes the largest. This shows that the new leader will grow in power and will eventually become the most powerful.

Daniel saw that the "horn had eyes like the eyes of a man and *a mouth that spoke boastfully*" (Dan. 7:8). We find a part of this description in the book of Revelation, where the apostle John tells what he saw in his vision: "The beast was given *a mouth to utter proud words* and blasphemies" (Rev. 13:5). It is apparent that the "horn" in the book of Daniel is the "beast" in the book of Revelation. The "beast" is otherwise known as the "Antichrist" (1 John 2:18).

THE BEAST AND HIS KINGDOM

In Revelation 13:1, John writes, "And I saw a beast coming out of the sea. He had ten horns." Here, we see the Antichrist arising.

As to the meaning of the ten horns, an angel explained this to John:

> The ten horns you saw are ten kings who have not yet received a kingdom, but who for one hour will receive authority as kings along with the beast. They have one purpose and will give their power and authority to the beast. (Rev. 17:12, 13)

These ten kings appear to be the same ten kings in Daniel's prophecy. After three of them are subdued (cf. Dan. 7:24), all ten will give their power to the Antichrist and form the core of his kingdom.

We gain more insight concerning the ten regents from Daniel 2. They are presented here in the form of ten toes on the feet of a statue the king of Babylon saw in a dream. Daniel received the interpretation of the dream and told it to the king:

> Just as you saw that the feet and toes were partly of baked clay and partly of iron, so this will be *a divided kingdom*; yet it will have some of the strength of iron in it, even as you saw iron mixed with clay. As the toes were partly iron and partly clay, so this kingdom will be partly strong and partly brittle. (Dan. 2:41, 42)

The coalition the Antichrist is going to lead will be "a divided kingdom." The kingdom will most probably be strong militarily, but at the same time have a weakness. This will perhaps be a lack of unity among the countries or people groups that comprise the kingdom. In Daniel 2:43 we read, "They will mingle with the seed of men; but they will not adhere to one another."

From Daniel 2:44 we see that the ten kings who are portrayed as the ten toes are in power until Jesus returns and sets up His kingdom: "And in the days of these kings the God of heaven will set up a kingdom which shall never be destroyed." The return of Christ and the setting up of His kingdom is shown in the prophecy in the form of a stone that smashes the feet on the statue and becomes a great mountain.

Chapter 6

The Growing Horn

The end time dictator is going to arise within the area that encompassed the ancient Roman Empire. We arrived at this fact in the last chapter. As to precisely where the Antichrist is going to arise, the book of Daniel gives us more information. We will start in the eighth chapter, where the prophet Daniel saw the shifting of kingdoms in the form of imagery:

> Suddenly a goat with a prominent horn between his eyes came from the west, crossing the whole earth without touching the ground. . . . The goat became very great, but at the height of his power his large horn was broken off, and in its place four prominent horns grew up toward the four winds of heaven. Out of one of them came *another horn, which started small* but grew in power to the south and to the east and toward the Beautiful Land. (Dan. 8:5, 8, 9)

In this prophecy, we meet again the little horn that we have identified as the Antichrist. We are told that he will originate from one of four horns. These horns grew up where a large horn belonging to a goat was broken off. Later in the chapter, we find the explanation:

The shaggy goat is the king of Greece, and the large horn between his eyes is the first king. (Dan. 8:21)

Undoubtedly, "the large horn" represents Alexander the Great, who founded the Grecian Empire in the fourth century B.C.

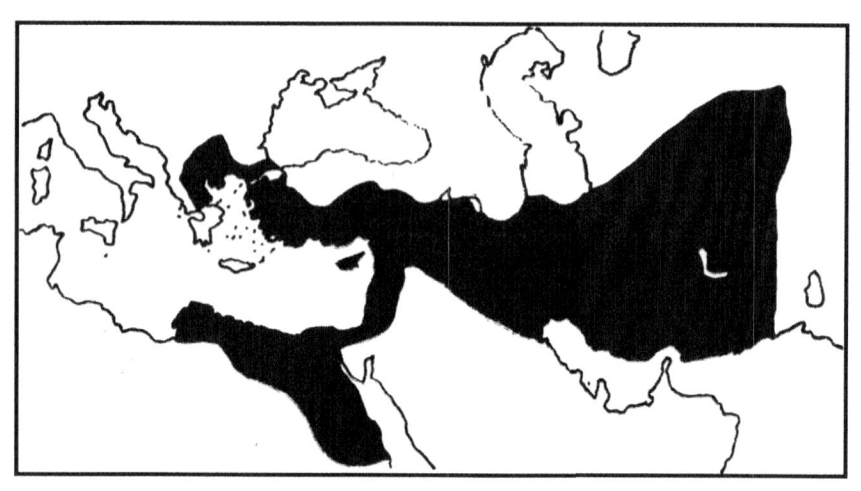

The Grecian Empire

FOUR—TWO—ONE

Let's look at the interpretation of the vision Daniel received concerning the Grecian Empire:

The four horns that replaced the one that was broken off represent four kingdoms that will emerge from his nation but will not have the same power. (Dan. 8:22)

After the death of Alexander the Great, four of his generals took over the kingdom. They divided it between themselves in four areas that generally correspond to 1. Greece; 2. Western Turkey; 3. Egypt, Lebanon, Cyprus, and Israel; 4. Syria, Central and Eastern Turkey, Iraq, Iran, Afghanistan, and Pakistan.

When we read, "Out of one of them came another horn,

which started small but grew in power" (Dan. 8:9), this seems to show that the "horn," i.e. the Antichrist, is going to arise from one of the four parts the ancient Grecian Empire was divided into.

Daniel 11 tells us which part. In the beginning of the chapter, we again read about the kingdom of Alexander the Great, which was broken up into four parts:

> Then a mighty king [Alexander the Great] will appear, who will rule with great power and do as he pleases. After he has appeared, his empire will be broken up and parceled out toward the four winds of heaven. (Dan. 11:3, 4)

The rest of the chapter concentrates on two of the four parts, right up to the time of the end. The two parts are "the South," which is Egypt (v.8) with adjacent areas, and "the North," which is Syria, also with adjacent areas. These phrases are used because of the geographical relation of the two kingdoms to the city of Jerusalem.

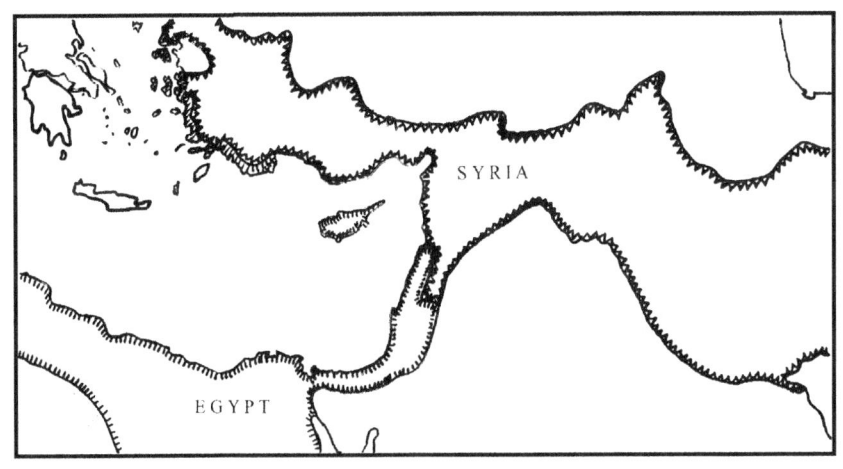

Syria and Egypt after the division of the Grecian Empire

Toward the end of Daniel 11, we read that "the king of the North" is going to perpetrate "the abomination that causes desolation" (v.31). According to what we have previously seen, "the abomination that causes desolation" will be perpetrated by the Antichrist. He is therefore "the king of the North." This suggests the Antichrist will come from within the area of ancient Syria, which comprises today of, among other countries, Syria, Turkey, and Iraq. These areas were not only a part of the Grecian Empire, but were later conquered by the Roman Empire—and as we have already ascertained, the little "horn," i.e. the Antichrist, will emerge from an area once dominated by the Romans (cf. Dan. 7:8).

Daniel 8:9 tells us the horn "which started small . . . grew in power to *the south* and to the east and toward the Beautiful Land [Israel]." To move southward, the starting point has to be in the north. This is another indication that the Antichrist will come from "the North," i.e. the Syrian division of the ancient Grecian Empire.

The origin of the Antichrist is also hinted at in Daniel 9. We are told here that a coming ruler will in the middle of a seven year period "put an end to sacrifice and offering" (v.27). As we have seen, this ruler is the Antichrist. Verse 26 tells us he will originate from the people who destroyed the temple in Jerusalem in 70 A.D.: "The people of the ruler who will come will destroy the city and the sanctuary." History informs us the tenth Roman legion that destroyed the temple, consisted of Syrian, Arabic, and Turkish recruits. This also shows that the Antichrist will arise in the Middle East.

ACCORDING TO THE WORK OF SATAN

The Antichrist will probably have functioned for some time as a regional politician or leader in the Middle East before he begins to draw attention to himself globally. The following prophecy is a descriptive explanation of the little horn that the angel Gabriel gave to Daniel:

> When rebels have become completely wicked, a stern-faced king, a master of intrigue, will arise. *He will become very strong, but not by his own power.* He will cause astounding

devastation and will succeed in whatever he does. He will destroy the mighty men and the holy people. He will cause deceit to prosper, and he will consider himself superior. When they feel secure, he will destroy many. (Dan. 8:23–25)

We see here that the power that makes the Antichrist very strong does not originate from himself. Revelation 13:2 says concerning the Antichrist, "The dragon gave the beast his power and his throne and great authority." Who "the dragon" is, can be seen from Revelation 12:9: "The great dragon was hurled down—that ancient serpent called the devil, or Satan, who leads the whole world astray." Paul's testimony agrees: "The coming of the lawless one is according to the working of Satan, with all power, signs, and lying wonders" (2 Thess. 2:9).

A wonder that will gain the world's attention and admiration is the Antichrist's "fatal wound" that is "healed" (Rev. 13:3). We are told the beast "was wounded by the sword and yet lived" (v.14). It is not clear what this entails, though a possible interpretation is an apparent resuscitation after an attempt on his life. It seems this will occur just prior to the great tribulation because according to Revelation 13:5, the Antichrist will proceed to "exercise his authority for forty-two months." This equals three and a half years, which we have seen is the length of the great tribulation.

People all over the world will be in ecstasy because of the Antichrist. They will exalt this man who is apparently invincible, and worship Satan who gives him authority:

> The whole world was astonished and followed the beast. Men worshiped the dragon because he had given authority to the beast, and they also worshiped the beast and asked, 'Who is like the beast? Who can make war against him?' (Rev. 13:3, 4)

Perhaps people will worship Satan without knowing it if he hides behind the name of a famed god. Of the Antichrist, we read in Daniel 11:37 & 38 that he will not respect God "nor regard any god; for he shall magnify himself above them all. But in their place he shall honor a *god of fortresses*," i.e. a god of war. The next verse says the Antichrist will greatly honor those who acknowledge this foreign god (v.39). We should consider the possibility that this points to the worship of the moon god Allah, who is associated with holy war.

The Antichrist not only "opposes and exalts himself above all that is called God or that is worshipped." He will also go as far as to show "himself that he is God" (2 Thess. 2:4), which implies he will probably give himself titles that belong to God alone. Moreover, because Islam is the dominant religion in the area where the Antichrist arises, it is not improbable that Muslims will be among the first to be given over to "a powerful delusion so that they will believe the lie" (2 Thess. 2:11). At present, Muslims number approximately one-fourth of the world's population.

Chapter 7

The Treaty and the Temple

When the Antichrist has risen to power he will make a certain treaty. The Bible says, "He shall confirm a covenant with many" (Dan. 9:27). According to the context of this verse, the treaty will involve the nation of Israel. It will most likely be a peace treaty for Israel and the Middle East.

Since the re-establishment of their national home in 1948, the Jews have constantly been in a state of preparedness for war because of hostile neighbors. In addition, there have been many protracted conflicts with Muslims in the autonomous areas within the country. Terror organizations in Gaza and Lebanon, backed by a menacing Iran, continue to be a threat. Israel is indeed in need of a lasting peace treaty.

FOCUS ON JERUSALEM

It is very probable that an important part of the treaty will concern Jerusalem, a city of central focus in end time prophecy, and a place that the worldwide media is preoccupied with. It is also possible that the treaty will precipitate the rebuilding of the temple in Jerusalem that was destroyed in 70 A.D. (unless it is built beforehand). That a new temple seems to be in the picture, can be seen by the mention of "sacrifice and offering" in the same verse that speaks of the covenant the Antichrist confirms. These offerings were an integral part of the Jewish temple service.

In the apostle John's vision of the great tribulation, the

temple is also mentioned:

> I was given a reed like a measuring rod and was told, Go and measure *the temple of God* and the altar, and count the worshipers there. But exclude the outer court; do not measure it, because it has been given to the Gentiles. They will trample on the holy city for 42 months. (Rev. 11:1, 2)

Here we see a rebuilt temple in the holy city of Jerusalem in the end time. The altar and worshipers are also mentioned. Notice that the area encompassing the outer court of the temple will be given to non-Jewish people. This implies the treaty could perhaps involve partial Muslim control over Jerusalem.

That a literal temple in Jerusalem is in view in these verses in Revelation 11 is supported by almost all the early church fathers. For example, Irenaeus wrote in about 185 A.D.:

> When this Antichrist has destroyed everything here in this world, he will reign three years and six months and sit in the temple in Jerusalem. And then the Lord will come from heaven on a cloud, in the glory of the Father. (Against Heresies, Book 5, chapter 30, verse 4)

PREPARATIONS FOR THE NEW TEMPLE

Ever since the Romans destroyed the temple in Jerusalem almost two thousand years ago, the Jews have had a desire to rebuild it. Religious Jews pray *Amidah* three times daily, a prayer that dates back to the time just after the destruction of the temple. It includes both a prayer for the return of the Jews to the land of Israel, as well as a prayer for the restoration of the temple sacrifices. On the Sabbath and on the feasts they pray an extra prayer for a swift rebuilding of the temple and renewed sacrifices.

In the days before Israel achieved independence in 1948, while former Prime Minister Menachem Begin was leader of Irgun (the Jewish Defense Force), he declared that one of their foremost goals in the Holy Land was to rebuild the temple.

Orthodox Jews around the world and especially those in Israel view the rebuilding of the temple as the most important way to bring Jews back to Judaism and preserve the Jewish people's identity.

The possibility of rebuilding the temple has existed ever since East Jerusalem and the Temple Mount were captured by Israel in 1967. Even though there have been some attempts to organize discussions about a rebuilding after 1967, it wasn't before the Palestinian uprising in 1987 that movements for the rebuilding of the temple began to organize themselves publicly. Fearing that either Arabic aggression or peaceful resolutions would deprive them of what they fought for in 1967, the number of groups with the goal of restoring the Temple Mount as a place of prayer for Jews began to grow. Today, there are many Jews who are eager to rebuild the temple, even though Israeli authorities do not give any official support. An opinion poll conducted in the summer of 2013 showed that one third of Israeli Jews want the holy temple to be rebuilt in Jerusalem.

Jews who are involved in preparations for the temple feel that the Jewish people live below the spiritual level God would have them on, and that this is the reason why the *shekina* (God's glory) is no longer present. Some of the religious Jews believe that the *shekina* is only present in the temple, and that the people cannot reach the desired spiritual level without the temple. They refer to the Jewish writing *Talmud* that says the temple will be built when the Messiah comes.

A well-known temple activist group in Israel today is *The Temple Mount and Eretz Yisrael Faithful Movement* (TMF). The most aggressive actions by TMF to promote the rebuilding of the temple are undoubtedly their attempts to lay the cornerstone of the temple. They made their first attempt in 1989, but the police prevented them from getting to the Temple Mount. Several other attempts have been made since, some of which have been violently opposed by the Palestinians.

A number of other Jewish groups in Jerusalem are now preparing men for service in the future restored temple. One of these groups, *Ateret Cohanim*, trains and educates temple priests. Another group, *The Temple Institute*, founded in Jerusalem in 1987, has made vessels that are planned for use in the future temple. Many instruments for worship in the temple are ready, as well as the priestly attire, and the holy incense. The inventory of the temple is now nearing completion.

THE TRIBULATION TEMPLE

A pressing issue is the question of where in Jerusalem the new temple will stand. This hinges on where the previous temple stood. Many assert it stood where the Dome of the Rock now stands on what is known as the Temple Mount.

However, certain scholars are of the opinion that the previous temple need not have stood where this Islamic shrine stands today. Dr. Asher Kaufman believes the previous temple stood north of the Dome of the Rock, while Mr. Bob Cornuke believes the temple stood south of this structure. If one of these theories is correct, this means the rebuilding of a new Jewish temple does not necessitate the removal of the Muslim Dome of the Rock.

Whatever the outcome concerning the precise location of the future temple, it will align with the prophecy in Revelation 11:2, which says, "The outer court . . . has been given to the Gentiles."

At present, preparations for the rebuilding of the temple are nearing completion. The will to construct is there, and knowledge of the precise site of the temple is forthcoming. Priests are in training, and temple vessels have been made. What remains is the political situation that will pave the way for the actual rebuilding to commence. The treaty of the Antichrist may well play a central role here.

Concerning the treaty, Daniel 9:27 says, "He shall confirm a covenant with many for one week [a "week" of years, i.e. seven years]." Then we read, "But in the middle of the week he shall bring an end to sacrifice and offering." This informs us that three and a half years after the treaty is signed (i.e. "in the middle of the week") the Antichrist will break it and stop the sacrificing in the new temple. The verse continues to say, "And on the wing of abominations shall be one who makes desolate." The Antichrist will be the one who "makes desolate" on the "wing of abominations." This is undoubtedly "the abomination that causes desolation," which we have seen triggers the great tribulation that lasts three and a half years.

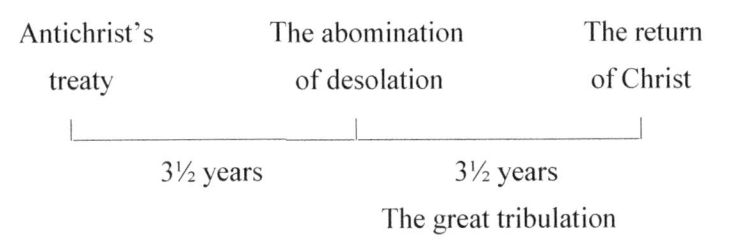

```
    Antichrist's         The abomination         The return
      treaty               of desolation         of Christ
    |_____|_____|
           3½ years              3½ years
                    The great tribulation
```

The period of great tribulation will run its course during the last half of the prophetic "week." These three and a half years correspond to the period non-Jews will "trample on" Jerusalem until Christ returns. The book of Revelation says: "The outer court . . . has been given to the Gentiles. They will trample on the holy city for 42 months" (Rev. 11:2).

THE RETURN TO THE LAND

The treaty that the Antichrist confirms with Israel, and the rebuilding of the Jewish temple, both have as their prerequisite the establishment of a Jewish state that encompasses Jerusalem. This became a reality in the 20th century after the Jews had wandered among the nations for more than eighteen hundred years.

The Hebrew prophets prophesied long ago of the regathering of the people of Israel back to their ancient homeland. Ezekiel was one of these prophets. He said:

Thus says the Lord God: 'Surely I will take the children of Israel from among the nations, wherever they have gone, and will gather them from every side and bring them into their own land; and I will make them one nation in the land, on the mountains of Israel.' (Ezek. 37:21, 22)

God said through the prophet Zechariah:

I will save My people from the land of the east and from the land of the west; I will bring them back, and they shall dwell in the midst of Jerusalem. (Zech. 8:7,8)

God spoke about the people of Israel also through the prophet Jeremiah, who wrote:

I will bring them back into their land which I gave to their fathers. (Jer. 16:15)

This prophecy aligns with what the psalmist wrote:

The Lord our God . . . remembers . . . the covenant which He made with Abraham, and His oath to Isaac, and confirmed it to Jacob for a statute, to Israel as an everlasting covenant, saying, 'To you I will give the land of Canaan as the allotment of your inheritance.' (Ps. 105:7–11, cf. Gen. 17:8, 26:3, 28:13)

The covenant concerning the Promised Land that God made with Abraham, Isaac, and Jacob (later renamed Israel, cf. Gen. 32:28), is eternal and unconditional, and therefore still effective. That there is today a state called Israel in the land where the fathers of the people of Israel dwelt is a sign that God has not gone back on His promise of giving the descendants of Jacob the land they are destined to inherit. It is also a sign that the scene is set for the fulfillment of end time prophecies, including the treaty of the Antichrist and the rebuilding of the temple in Jerusalem.

Part 3

During the Tribulation

Chapter 8

The Kingdom of the Beast

It is generally asserted that during the great tribulation the Antichrist will have control over absolutely every country in the world. This assertion is based on the following passages: "All the world marveled and followed the beast" (Rev. 13:3); "And he was given authority over every tribe, people, language, and nation" (Rev. 13:7); "And all who dwell on the earth will worship him" (Rev. 13:8). Yet if we compare these verses with other Scripture references of a similar nature, we may arrive at another understanding.

In Daniel 2:37 & 38 the prophet Daniel said to Nebuchadnezzar, the king of Babylon:

> You, O king, are the king of kings. The God of heaven has given you dominion and power and might and glory; in your hands he has placed mankind and the beasts of the field and the birds of the air. *Wherever* they live, he has made you ruler over them *all*.

In the next chapter, we read the following:

> Therefore, as soon as they heard the sound of the horn, flute, zither, lyre, harp and all kinds of music, *all the peoples, nations and men of every language* fell down and worshiped the image of gold that King Nebuchadnezzar had set up. (Dan. 3:7)

Daniel said the following to Belshazzar who was also a king of Babylon:

> O king, the Most High God gave your father Nebuchadnezzar sovereignty and greatness and glory and splendor. Because of the high position he gave him, *all the peoples and nations and men of every language* dreaded and feared him. (Dan. 5:18, 19)

The book of Daniel is not the only book in the Bible that gives us the impression that Nebuchadnezzar reigned over the whole world. We read in Jeremiah 34:1 about "Nebuchadnezzar king of Babylon . . . and *all the kingdoms of the earth* that were under his dominion" (ASV). History tells us, however, that Nebuchadnezzar never reigned over the great Chinese kingdom of that time, nor over the civilizations in India, Greece, and Italy. The vast expanses of North- and South America, Europe, Africa, and Asia were not subjected to Nebuchadnezzar.

The Babylonian Empire

What is then meant by "all the kingdoms of the earth," "all" people "wherever they live" and "all the peoples, nations and men of every language" in the verses above? In biblical terminology it is those within the Babylonian Empire who are referred to, because that was all Nebuchadnezzar reigned over. Similar language is used of the Medo-Persian Empire. In 2 Chronicles 36:23 we read, "This is what Cyrus king of Persia says: The Lord, the God of heaven, has given me *all the kingdoms of the earth.*" Likewise, Daniel 6:25 says, "Then king Darius wrote unto *all the peoples, nations, and languages, that dwell in all the earth.*"

The Medo-Persian Empire

The Bible also shows that Alexander the Great reigned "over *all the earth*" (Dan. 2:39), but only the Grecian Empire is spoken of here. This empire was larger than the Babylonian Empire, and can be compared to the extent of the Medo-Persian Empire, but was small in relation to the entire globe.

The Grecian Empire

In Luke 2:1, we read that "there went out a decree from Caesar Augustus, that *all the world* should be enrolled" (ASV). Augustus was Caesar in the Roman Empire, but neither did he reign over North- and South America, India, China, and other large areas of land. The biblical expression "all the world" is therefore a limited expression and only designates the extent of the Roman Empire.

The Roman Empire

ANTICHRIST'S EXTENT OF POWER

How then are we to understand the statement in Revelation 13:7, which says the Antichrist will be "given authority over every tribe, people, language and nation"? We have seen that similar language is used of the Babylonian Empire, the Medo-Persian Empire, the Grecian Empire, and the Roman Empire. This implies that the Antichrist will only have authority over the people who will be under his control, in the same way as Nebuchadnezzar, Cyrus, Darius, Alexander the Great, and Augustus only had power over those who were within the borders of their empires. It is all a question of the extent of Antichrist's "kingdom" (Rev. 16:10).

According to what we have arrived at in previous chapters, the Antichrist seems to appear in the Middle East. He will arise among ten regional leaders who "will give their power and authority to the beast" (Rev. 17:12, 13). These ten leaders will constitute the platform of power in his kingdom. However, Antichrist's fame and influence is going to spread after he recovers from his deadly wound. We are told in Revelation 13:3: "His deadly wound was healed. And all the world marveled and followed the beast." Then we read, "And all who dwell on the earth will worship him, whose names have not been written in the Book of Life" (Rev. 13:8). The Antichrist will be admired, followed, and worshipped by all, except the believers. Hence, he will gain authority over the peoples of the earth.

However, the biblical material we have looked at shows that he will not necessarily have direct control of every single country in the world. One country that will not be under the Antichrist is alluded to in Daniel 11:41: "Many countries will fall, but Edom, Moab and the leaders of Ammon will be delivered from his hand." The biblical areas depicted here comprise the land of Jordan today. Since this country will escape the Antichrist's grasp, there is a good possibility that also other countries will not come under his rule.

In the continuation of the prophecy in Daniel 11, we read of the Antichrist:

He shall stretch out his hand against the countries, and the land of Egypt shall not escape. . . . But news *from the east* and the north shall trouble him, therefore he shall go out with great fury to destroy and annihilate many. (Dan. 11:42, 44)

Here we see the Antichrist taking over countries and gaining enemies in the course of the tribulation period. Those "from the east" are probably "the kings from the east" (Rev. 16:12) who send their armies against the Antichrist. The implication here is that he will not have control of absolutely every country in the world.

THE KINGS OF THE EARTH

Even if the Antichrist's control is not totally global, he will have significant influence on the whole world. He will be aided by "spirits of demons performing miraculous signs, and they go out to the kings of the whole world, to gather them" (Rev. 16:14). The Antichrist will be able to influence these state leaders, but we are not told whether they will "give their power and authority to the beast," as the ten rulers do.

In fact, there will be dissent between the ten rulers and other leaders in the world. This will be apparent in their relation to "the great city Babylon" (Rev. 18:21). In Revelation 17:16 it says that the Antichrist and the ten rulers "will hate the prostitute [Babylon] . . . bring her to ruin . . . and burn her with fire." The other rulers on the earth will lament because of her destruction: "When the kings of the earth who committed adultery with her and shared her luxury see the smoke of her burning, they will weep and mourn over her" (Rev. 18:9).

As to what extent the Antichrist is going to gain authority over the nations of the world and their leaders, only time will tell. Yet one thing seems to be clear in light of the prophecies; the Antichrist first controls ten leaders, apparently in the Middle East. He then gains extended power at the time of the great tribulation.

Chapter 9

The Decree of the False Prophet

The book of Revelation uses the term "beast" of the Antichrist. He is, however, not the only one called a beast in this prophetic book. We read of "another beast" assisting him (Rev. 13:11). Let's take a look at what this individual is going to do:

> He exercised all the authority of the first beast on his behalf, and made the earth and its inhabitants worship the first beast, whose fatal wound had been healed. And he performed great and miraculous signs, even causing fire to come down from heaven to earth in full view of men. Because of the signs he was given power to do on behalf of the first beast, he deceived the inhabitants of the earth. He ordered them to set up an image in honor of the beast who was wounded by the sword and yet lived. He was given power to give breath to the image of the first beast, so that it could speak and cause all who refused to worship the image to be killed. (Rev. 13:12–15)

While the Antichrist is presented as a political leader, the second "beast" will apparently be a religious leader. He is also called "the false prophet" (Rev. 19:20), and will be able to perform "great and miraculous signs" (Rev. 13:13). We read that he will speak "like a dragon" (Rev. 13:11), which according to Revelation 12:9 refers to the Devil. This Satan-inspired man will deceive "the inhabitants of the earth" (v.14) and command the worship of a speaking image of the Antichrist. He sees to it that those who refuse to worship this image pay with their lives.

MARKED OR NOT MARKED

The false prophet is going to introduce a system that not only makes a new order possible, but also ensures that those who are outside of the system are handed over to hunger and want:

> He also forced everyone, small and great, rich and poor, free and slave, to receive a mark on his right hand or on his forehead, so that no one could buy or sell unless he had the mark, which is the name of the beast or the number of his name. This calls for wisdom. If anyone has insight, let him calculate the number of the beast, for it is man's number. His number is 666. (Rev. 13:16–18)

How are we to understand the "mark" that everyone must have on his right hand or on his forehead in order to buy or sell? Apparently, the enforcement of the mark of the beast presupposes a central system that controls each individual's right to subsist. This system will perhaps involve computerized financial transactions. Today's technology allows this to be carried out by means of microchips implanted under the skin. When the time comes, the false prophet could make use of such a system to exercise complete control on behalf of the Antichrist. Otherwise, the "mark" could simply be a visible sign permanently etched on the skin, or else just covering the skin. In any case, the result will be the same—no trade without being subject to the system.

The mark of the beast is referred to with great seriousness. The Bible gives strong warnings against being seduced into receiving it:

> Then a third angel followed them, saying with a loud voice, 'If anyone worships the beast and his image, and receives his mark on his forehead or on his hand, he himself shall also drink of the wine of the wrath of God, which is poured out full

strength into the cup of His indignation. He shall be tormented with fire and brimstone in the presence of the holy angels and in the presence of the Lamb. And the smoke of their torment ascends forever and ever; and they have no rest day or night, who worship the beast and his image, and whoever receives the mark of his name.' (Rev. 14:9–11)

The false prophet's intention will be to cause all who refuse to worship "the beast and his image" to be killed (Rev. 13:15). Since worshipping the Antichrist and receiving his mark are tied together (cf. Rev. 14:9), we can assume that refusing to receive the mark will be regarded as refusing to worship the Antichrist. Those who do not submit to the Antichrist will be sentenced to death.

Will all those who do not receive the mark be killed? The Bible shows that the answer must be no. At Christ's judgment of the nations that takes place when He returns there will be righteous people still alive who enter into the kingdom (Matt. 25:31–46). In addition, Zechariah 14 tells us there will be many from different nations who are alive and enter into the kingdom that will be established when Christ returns (v.3, 4, 9, 16–19). None of these will receive the mark, because if they do they cannot enter into the kingdom. Perhaps people from certain nations not under the Antichrist are included here, but definitely people who have lived in hiding within his realm. We can safely say that even though many will be killed, there will be others who manage to escape death.

PERSECUTION OF THE SAINTS

The majority of those who refuse to receive the mark will be believers in Jesus. The Antichrist will be enraged at them because they will not bow to him. He will then "make war against the saints" (Rev. 13:7). The next verse reveals who these saints are. They are those whose names are "written in the book of life belonging to the Lamb that was slain" (Rev. 13:8).

How this war will be waged is stated a couple of verses later, where we read of those who "go into captivity" and those who will be "killed with the sword" (Rev. 13:10). Many are going to die by being beheaded. After the tribulation period, the apostle John sees those who had been killed:

> And I saw the souls of those who had been *beheaded* because of their testimony for Jesus and because of the word of God. They had not worshiped the beast or his image and had not received his mark on their foreheads or their hands. (Rev. 20:4)

Beheading is a form of execution used by Muslim extremists. This is an indication that fundamentalist Islam, which in its purest form is both anti-Semitic and anti-Christian, could very well be the Antichrist's system of government.

The saints will have to stand firm. Hence, we read in the last part of Revelation 13:10, where "captivity" and "sword" are mentioned: "This calls for patient endurance and faithfulness on the part of the saints." What is said here aligns with Revelation 14:12 that follows the warning against receiving the mark of the Antichrist: "This calls for patient endurance on the part of the saints who obey God's commandments and remain faithful to Jesus."

As we have already noted, the Antichrist will "exercise his authority for forty-two months" (Rev. 13:5). This is equivalent to three and a half years, and is the length of time the Antichrist will oppress the saints of God:

> He will speak out against the Most High and wear down the saints of the Highest One . . . and they will be given into his hand for a time, times, and half a time. (Dan. 7:25)

During his reign of terror, the Antichrist is going to persecute the saints with all means at his disposal. He will use betrayal (Matt. 24:10), imprisonment and torture (Rev. 2:10), as well as executions (Rev. 20:4). The saints' activity will be forbidden, they will be forced to go underground, and many will be martyred.

THE FIFTH SEAL AND THE SLAIN

In an earlier chapter, we noted what the apostle John saw when the first four seals in the book of Revelation are opened. When the next seal is opened, he sees martyrs:

When He opened the fifth seal, I saw under the altar the souls of those who had been slain because of the word of God and the testimony they had maintained. (Rev. 6:9)

This aligns with what Jesus says concerning His disciples in His end time discourse:

Then you will be handed over to be persecuted and put to death, and you will be hated by all nations because of me. (Matt. 24:9)

He also foretold the following about the believers:

You will be betrayed even by parents, brothers, relatives and friends, and they will put some of you to death. All men will hate you because of me. But not a hair of your head will perish. By standing firm you will gain life. (Luke 21:16–19)

Today there is growing opposition against those who believe in Jesus. Of the fifty countries in the world where faith in Christ costs the most, three-quarters are Muslim countries. Believers are discriminated, maltreated, imprisoned, ousted, and killed. This will only increase as we approach the end of the age.

Chapter 10

Saints in the Tribulation

People who believe in Jesus will be present in the great tribulation. This fact is indisputable, as the previous chapter has shown. The question is whether all these people become believers after the beginning of the great tribulation. This is not an insignificant detail because many claim that Jesus will fetch His church to heaven before the great tribulation, and that the believers we read about in the great tribulation belong to another group.

As to whether the church is in heaven during the great tribulation or not, is dealt with in detail in section two. For now, we shall only look at a few points that shed light on this matter.

CHRIST'S END TIME DISCOURSE

Jesus spoke about the last days in a number of passages including Matthew 24 and Mark 13. In these two chapters, He spoke about the time both before, during, and after the great tribulation. If we can ascertain whom Jesus spoke to, and whom He spoke of, then we will be able to clear up the issue of whether or not the end time believers are to be divided into two groups, i.e. on the one hand the church, and on the other, believers in the great tribulation.

In Matthew 24:3, we see that Jesus was speaking to His disciples. Mark 13:3 gives us their names: Peter, James, John, and Andrew. Jesus said "you" many times in His discourse. Evidently, He was referring to His first disciples, but also to future disciples, since the first disciples of Christ died without seeing everything fulfilled. In Matthew 24, Jesus said "you" and "your" seventeen times—seven times before He mentioned the "great tribulation" (v.21), three times during the tribulation, and seven times afterward. In Mark 13, Jesus said the words "you" and "your" twenty-one times—ten times before He mentioned the great tribulation (v.19), three times in the course of the tribulation period, and eight times afterward. Jesus directed the whole of His end time discourse to His disciples, and made no difference between disciples living before the great tribulation and disciples present in the great tribulation. Disciples are present on the earth until Christ comes in glory after this time (Matt. 24:29, 30; Mark 13:24, 25).

According to the teaching of Jesus, there is no cause to divide the believers in the end time into two groups, and say that some of the disciples are the church, and some belong to another group in the great tribulation. On the contrary, we see one flock of disciples that Jesus calls "My church" in Matthew 16:18.

Some make a point of the fact that the disciples Jesus spoke to were Jews, and that He therefore spoke of the Jews in the end time. However, we have to remember that Peter and John, who were among those Jesus spoke to on this occasion, were regarded as "pillars" in Christ's church (Gal. 2:9). All the early believers in the church were Jews, and only later did non-Jewish people become believers and thus a part of the church. In 1 Corinthians 12:13 we read:

> For we were all baptized by one Spirit so as to form one body—whether Jews or Gentiles.

Many Gentiles were saved, especially through the ministry of Paul, and soon they became a majority in the church. We must therefore conclude that Jesus directed His end time discourse to the whole of His church, i.e. believers of both Jewish and Gentile lineage.

CHRIST'S ELECT

Besides using the words "you" and "your," Jesus also employed the phrase "the elect." They will be present in the end time (Matt. 24:24). In verse 32, we find the expression "*His* elect." The word "His" refers to "the Son of Man" (v.30), i.e. Jesus. This tells us that "the elect" are Christ's elect.

Who are Christ's elect? In Mark's version of Christ's end time discourse, we also find the expression "the elect" (Mark 13:20). Jesus defines them in the same verse as those "whom He has chosen." This aligns with what Jesus said to His disciples in John 15:19: "I have *chosen* you out of the world." The elect are therefore followers of Jesus.

The apostle Peter wrote to believers and called them "elect" (1 Pet. 1:2). Also the apostle Paul addressed the believers as "the elect of God" (Col. 3:12). This is, of course, a reference to the church. Therefore, when Jesus spoke of His elect in Matthew 24, He was referring to His church. Accordingly, the elect of Christ are synonymous with the church of Christ, which He said He would build (Matt. 16:18).

By closely examining Christ's discourse in Matthew 24, we see that the expressions "the elect" and "His elect" are connected to the word "you," which we have seen occurs many times in the chapter. As shown, the word "you" refers primarily to the disciples of Jesus who were sitting on the Mount of Olives and listening to Him on this occasion. The three times the word "elect" occur are followed up in the next verse by the word "you" in a way that equates the two words. This shows the elect of Christ include both the disciples who witnessed His death and resurrection, as well as people from "all nations" in "the whole world" (Matt. 24:14) who would become believers. We see this expressed in Christ's prayer in John 17:20: "My prayer is not for them [the eleven] alone. I pray also for those who will believe in me through their message." All those who believe in Jesus are "His elect" (Matt. 24:31), and they comprise His church.

Jesus said concerning His elect and the great tribulation:

> If those days had not been cut short, no one would survive, but for the sake of *the elect* those days will be shortened. (Matt.

24:22)

In other words, the great tribulation will be short for the sake of the church. What Jesus says here is difficult to comprehend if the church will be transferred to heaven beforehand.

THE SAINTS

When we study the book of Revelation, we discover the same as what Jesus showed in His end time discourse concerning the church. The great tribulation seems to be depicted in chapters 6–18, and in these chapters, we find people present called "the saints." In Revelation 14:12, we read about "*the saints* who obey *God's commandments* and remain faithful to Jesus." These are referred to in chapter 12 as "those who obey *God's commandments* and hold to *the testimony* of Jesus" (v.17). Those who are martyred among them are portrayed in chapter 6 as "those who had been slain because of *the word of God* and *the testimony* they had maintained" (v.9).

In these references we see that "God's commandments" are equated with "the word of God," and that both these expressions are connected to "the testimony of Jesus." The author of the book of Revelation also wrote about "the testimony" in 1 John 5:9–11, and about keeping God's commandments (1 John 2:3, 4, 7, 8; 3:22–24; 4:21; 5:2, 3). He says that doing what God commands is the same as obeying God's word (1 John 2:4, 5). This was written to believers in the church. We have therefore every reason to believe that "the saints who obey God's commandments and remain faithful to Jesus" in Revelation 14 are believers in the church.

The saints are also mentioned elsewhere in the book of Revelation:

> He was given power to make war against *the saints*. . . . If anyone is to go into captivity, into captivity he will go. If anyone is to be killed with the sword, with the sword he will be killed. This calls for patient endurance and faithfulness on the part of *the saints*. (Rev. 13:7, 10)

In Revelation 17:6 we read, "I saw the woman, drunk with the blood of *the saints*." Paul uses the same expression—"the saints" multiple times in his letters to denote believers who comprise the church. Therefore, in view of this, there isn't anything in the book of Revelation to give the impression that the saints here are other than the saints who make up the universal church.

Summary: From what we have looked at, we conclude that the believers in the great tribulation are not a separate group outside of the church. We do not therefore see any reason to believe that the church will be fetched to heaven before the great tribulation.

Chapter 11

The Woman and the Witnesses

The book of Revelation contains certain signs that tell us about what will happen in the end time. One such sign can be found in chapter 12, verse 1. Here we read:

> A great and wondrous sign appeared in heaven: a woman clothed with *the sun*, with *the moon* under her feet and a crown of *twelve stars* on her head.

We find this symbolism also in Genesis 37:9 & 10, where we read about Joseph's dream:

> Then he had another dream, and he told it to his brothers. 'Listen,' he said, 'I had another dream, and this time *the sun and moon and eleven stars* were bowing down to me.' When he told his father as well as his brothers, his father rebuked him and said, 'What is this dream you had? Will *your mother and I and your brothers* actually come and bow down to the ground before you?'

Jacob, Joseph's father, understood the meaning of the dream, and interpreted it correctly. The sun was Jacob, the moon portrayed Rachel Joseph's mother, and the eleven stars represented Joseph's eleven brothers. It seems probable that the twelfth star in Revelation 12 can be connected to Joseph himself.

God gave Jacob a new name, Israel (cf. Gen. 32:28), and his sons were the origin of the twelve tribes of Israel. Later in the Bible, the people of Israel are collectively portrayed as a woman (cf. Is. 54; Jer. 3; Ezek. 16; Hos. 2; etc.). With this background in view, we can be sure that the "woman" in Revelation 12 is associated with the people of Israel. They are the people that Jesus was born among. Revelation 12:5 says, "She gave birth to a son, a male child, who will rule all the nations with an iron scepter."

That the people of Israel are in the picture is also supported by Revelation 12:7. Here, the archangel Michael and his angels fight against the dragon that is then thrown down to the earth. The same archangel is mentioned in Daniel 12:1, where we read of "Michael, the great prince who protects your people." The expression "your people" refers to the prophet Daniel's people, which are the Jews. After mentioning Michael, the first verse in Daniel 12 continues: "And there shall be a time of trouble, such as never was since there was a nation, even to that time." This is the time of the great tribulation.

THE WOMAN IN THE DESERT

At the beginning of the great tribulation, the "woman" will seek refuge:

> The woman fled into the desert to a place prepared for her by God, where she might be taken care of for 1,260 days. (Rev. 12:6)

The 1,260 days the "woman" spends in the desert equals three and a half years, which we have seen is the length of the great tribulation.

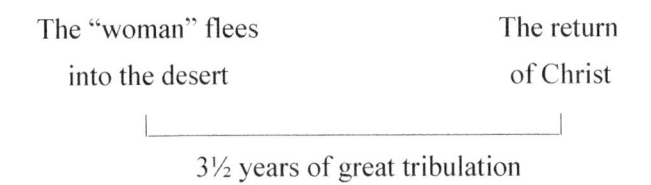

```
The "woman" flees                The return
   into the desert                of Christ
          |_____|
              3½ years of great tribulation
```

We find the reason why the "woman" has to flee into the desert later in the chapter:

> The great dragon was hurled down—that ancient serpent called the devil, or Satan, who leads the whole world astray. He was hurled to the earth, and his angels with him. . . . When the dragon saw that he had been hurled to the earth, he pursued the woman who had given birth to the male child. The woman was given the two wings of a great eagle, so that she might fly to the place prepared for her in the desert, where she would be taken care of for a time, times and half a time, out of the serpent's reach. (Rev. 12:9, 13, 14)

In another end time prophecy, we read of the Antichrist: "He will also invade the Beautiful Land" (Dan. 11:41). Incited by Satan, the Antichrist will enter the land of Israel, and as we have seen, desecrate the temple in Jerusalem. Jesus said that when His disciples see this "abomination of desolation" happen "then let those who are *in Judea* flee to the mountains" (Matt. 24:15, 16). He also said to His disciples: "And pray that *your* flight may not be in winter or on the Sabbath. For then there will be great tribulation" (vv.20, 21). It appears therefore the "woman" symbolizes end time disciples of Jesus in Israel (in the area of ancient Judea) who flee for safety at the start of the great tribulation. God is going to protect a believing remnant from Israel in a "place prepared for her in the desert" (Rev. 12:14).

Where will this be? The continuation of Daniel 11:41 says, "Many countries will fall, but Edom, Moab and the leaders of Ammon will be delivered from his hand." God is going to make sure the Antichrist will not lay hold of the biblical lands of

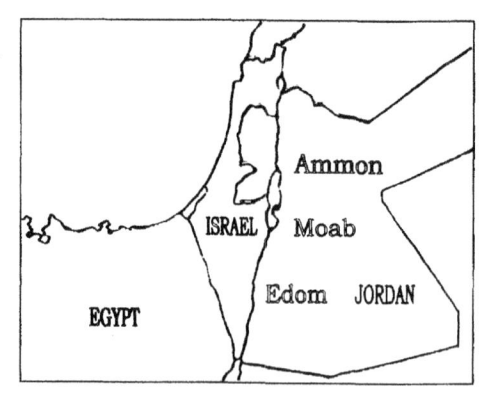

Edom, Moab, and Ammon. These comprise parts of the country of Jordan today.

It is therefore probable that the place of refuge will be somewhere in Jordan. This could be what is mirrored in the prophecy of Isaiah 16:4: "Let My outcasts dwell with you, O Moab; be a shelter to them from the face of the spoiler."

According to the apostle John, the contingent of believers from Israel who find their way to the place of refuge will receive God's provision for all that is necessary for their survival in the course of the great tribulation.

DOUBLE DOSE

At the same time as the flight into the desert takes place, two prophets of the Lord will step forward. They will prophesy daily and perform signs during the three and a half years of the great tribulation without anyone being able to stop them (Rev. 11:3–5). Their testimony will be broadcasted to the whole world, and they will be a thorn in the Antichrist's eye.

The Antichrist will eventually succeed in killing them in Jerusalem. The whole world will see their bodies lying in the street, presumably on satellite TV. Many will celebrate the occasion. After three days the two witnesses will, in the same way as their Lord, be raised from the dead, and thereafter received up into heaven. A terrible earthquake will then hit Jerusalem, and the time for the return of Christ will have come.

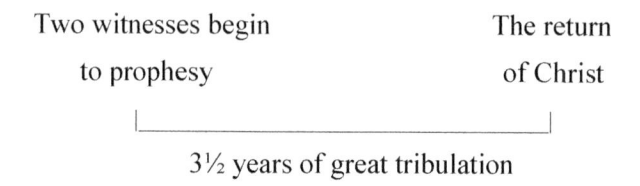

Two witnesses begin to prophesy		The return of Christ
	———————————————	
	3½ years of great tribulation	

The book of Revelation relates the events that will happen:

> And I will give power to My two witnesses, and they will prophesy for 1,260 days, clothed in sackcloth. These are the two olive trees and the two lampstands that stand before the Lord of the earth. If anyone tries to harm them, fire comes from their mouths and devours their enemies. This is how anyone who wants to harm them must die.
>
> These men have power to shut up the sky so that it will not rain during the time they are prophesying; and they have power to turn the waters into blood and to strike the earth with every kind of plague as often as they want.
>
> Now when they have finished their testimony, the beast that comes up from the Abyss will attack them, and overpower and kill them. Their bodies will lie in the street of the great city, which is figuratively called Sodom and Egypt, where also their Lord was crucified. For three and a half days men from every people, tribe, language and nation will gaze on their bodies and refuse them burial. The inhabitants of the earth will gloat over them and will celebrate by sending each other gifts, because these two prophets had tormented those who live on the earth.
>
> But after the three and a half days a breath of life from God entered them, and they stood on their feet, and terror struck those who saw them. Then they heard a loud voice from heaven saying to them, 'Come up here.' And they went up to heaven in a cloud, while their enemies looked on.
>
> At that very hour there was a severe earthquake and a tenth of the city collapsed. Seven thousand people were killed in the earthquake, and the survivors were terrified and gave glory to the God of heaven. (Rev. 11:3–13)

As to the nature of the ministry of the two witnesses, it seems likely they will prepare the people of God for the second coming of Christ as John the Baptist prepared the people for Christ's appearance at His first coming. They will most probably be calling people to repentance and faith.

Chapter 12

Death and Destruction

In the great tribulation, it will look as if the world has come off its hinges. Jesus said, "There will be . . . fearful events and great signs from heaven" (Luke 21:11). He also said, "On the earth, nations will be in anguish" (Luke 21:25). We find details of what will happen in the book of Revelation:

> Hail and fire followed, mingled with blood, and they were thrown to the earth. And a third of the trees were burned up, and all green grass was burned up. . . .
> And something like a great mountain burning with fire was thrown into the sea, and a third of the sea became blood. And a third of the living creatures in the sea died, and a third of the ships were destroyed. . . .
> And a great star fell from heaven, burning like a torch, and it fell on a third of the rivers and on the springs of water. The name of the star is Wormwood. A third of the waters became wormwood, and many men died from the water, because it was made bitter. (Rev. 8:7–11)

The environmental catastrophe will be complete:

> The sea . . . became blood as of a dead man, and every living creature in the sea died. . . . The rivers and springs of water . . . became blood. (Rev. 16:3, 4)

There will be atmospheric changes for the worse:

> A third of the sun was struck, a third of the moon, and a third of the stars, so that a third of them turned dark. A third of the day was without light, and also a third of the night. (Rev. 8:12)

Large earthquakes will also mark the last days:

> At that very hour there was a severe earthquake. (Rev. 11:13)

> There was a great earthquake, such as there had not been since man came to be upon the earth. (Rev. 16:18)

It is imperative that end time believers follow Jesus' instructions to avoid the calamities that will occur before He comes back. The Lord said, "Pray that you may be able to escape all that is about to happen, and that you may be able to stand before the Son of Man" (Luke 21:36). He also said, "By standing firm you will gain life" (Luke 21:19).

THE SUFFERING OF THE UNGODLY

According to Revelation 9, hordes of horrible winged creatures will be let loose and torment people who do not belong to God, and who are therefore without protection:

> They were not given power to kill them, but only to torture them for five months. And the agony they suffered was like that of the sting of a scorpion when it strikes a man. During those days men will seek death, but will not find it; they will long to die, but death will elude them. (vv.5, 6)

God is going to punish those who worship the Antichrist, and refuse to repent of their evil ways and their blasphemy:

Ugly and painful sores broke out on the people who had the mark of the beast and worshiped his image....

... The sun was given power to scorch people with fire. They were seared by the intense heat and they cursed the name of God, who had control over these plagues, but they refused to repent and glorify Him.

... His [Antichrist's] kingdom was plunged into darkness. Men gnawed their tongues in agony and cursed the God of heaven because of their pains and their sores, but they refused to repent of what they had done....

From the sky huge hailstones of about a hundred pounds each fell upon men. And they cursed God on account of the plague of hail, because the plague was so terrible. (Rev. 16:2, 8–11, 21)

ARMAGEDDON

Toward the end of the great tribulation, the Antichrist and the false prophet are going to demonically influence "the kings of the whole world" (Rev. 16:14) in order to gather them together. Their motive will be to finish off Israel once and for all, and eradicate Jews in Jerusalem. The Lord says through the prophet Zechariah: "When all the nations of the earth are gathered against her, I will make Jerusalem an immovable rock for all the nations" (Zech. 12:3).

When the nations of the world send their armies against the Holy Land, the water in the great river Euphrates will be "dried up to prepare the way for the kings from the East" (Rev. 16:12).

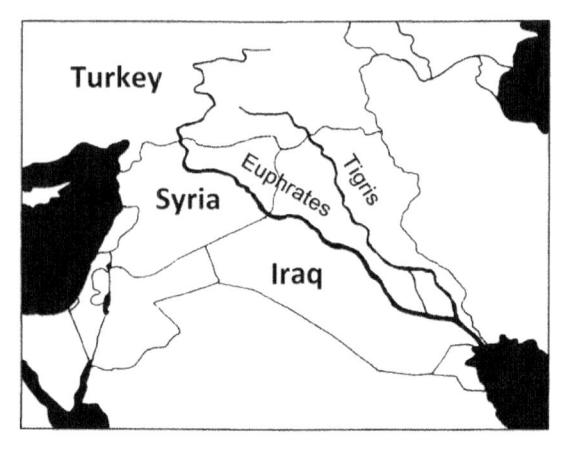

The source of the great river Euphrates lies in the Armenian highlands. It flows through Turkey and Syria, then into Iraq where it joins the river Tigris, and runs into the sea in the Persian Gulf. It literally divides the landscape in two, and with a length of almost 1750 miles, it is the longest river in the Middle East. The river Euphrates has traditionally been regarded as the dividing line between the Near East and the Far East. The Turks have built large dams across the river, and are able to stop the water supply and thereby lay the riverbed dry. When the river is dried up then the way will be clear for the armies from the East.

Besides the forces from the East, "the kings of the whole world" will be gathered "for the battle on the great day of God Almighty" (Rev. 16:14). Verse 16 says, "Then they gathered the kings together to the place that in Hebrew is called Armageddon." Armageddon is a compound Hebrew expression, formed of the word "ar," which means "hill," and "Megiddo," a place in Northern Israel. The hill of Megiddo is situated near the Mediterranean Sea. From the top there is a view across a large valley that stretches eastwards. This valley is 14 miles wide and 20 miles long, and will most probably be the gathering place for the armies of the world before they march on Jerusalem.

An enormous amount of people will die in the ensuing carnage: "A third of mankind was killed by the three plagues of fire, smoke and sulfur" (Rev. 9:18). It is apparent this will happen in the space of just one hour (cf. Rev. 9:15). Weapons of mass destruction will clearly be used. It will be a war of nuclear inferno, biological holocaust, and chemical catastrophe that will bring mankind to the brink of the precipice.

Part 4

After the Tribulation

Chapter 13

The Revelation of the Redeemer

When it looks as dark as it can get, and war threatens to extinguish life on the earth, God is going to intervene. To begin with, there will be great cosmic signs. Jesus told about this in His end time discourse:

> Immediately after the tribulation of those days the sun will be darkened, and the moon will not give its light; the stars will fall from heaven, and the powers of the heavens will be shaken. (Matt. 24:29)

A solar eclipse and a lunar eclipse will occur. The whole cosmos will look as if it is breaking up, and the earth will shudder, as the Lord says in Isaiah 13:13: "I will shake the heavens, and the earth shall remove out of her place." In the book of Revelation, we read:

> Then there came flashes of lightning, rumblings, peals of thunder and a severe earthquake. No earthquake like it has ever occurred since man has been on earth, so tremendous was the quake. The great city split into three parts, and the cities of the nations collapsed. (Rev. 16:18, 19)

This massive earthquake will cause enormous tidal waves. The devastation will be so vast that people all over the world will react with dread, as Jesus said they would:

> There will be signs in the sun, moon and stars. On the earth, nations will be in anguish and perplexity at the roaring and tossing of the sea. Men will faint from terror, apprehensive of what is coming on the world, for the heavenly bodies will be shaken. (Luke 21:25, 26)

In the terrifying darkness and enormous chaos, a great light will suddenly shine high in the sky. The whole world will see the glory of the Lord Jesus Christ as He descends from heaven. Jesus Himself put it this way:

> At that time the sign of the Son of Man will appear in the sky, and all the nations of the earth will mourn. They will see the Son of Man coming on the clouds of the sky, with power and great glory. (Matt. 24:30)

DESPERATION AND REDEMPTION

The apostle John describes the return of Christ like this:

> Look, He is coming with the clouds, and every eye will see Him, even those who pierced Him; and all the peoples of the earth will mourn because of Him. So shall it be! Amen. (Rev. 1:7)

People across the entire globe will be horrified and cry in despair when they see what is happening. Many will seek refuge in an attempt to hide themselves from God. The following is a vivid portrayal of the awful events to come:

> There was a great earthquake. The sun turned black like sackcloth made of goat hair, the whole moon turned blood red,

and the stars in the sky fell to earth, as late figs drop from a fig tree when shaken by a strong wind. The sky receded like a scroll rolling up, and every mountain and island was removed from its place. . . .

Then the kings of the earth, the princes, the generals, the rich, the mighty, and every slave and every free man hid in caves and among the rocks of the mountains. They called to the mountains and the rocks, 'Fall on us and hide us from the face of Him who sits on the throne and from the wrath of the Lamb! For the great day of their wrath has come, and who can stand?' (Rev. 6:12–17)

Those who have longed for the return of Christ are going to react in a completely different way. The believers will rejoice, because now the greatest moment of their lives has come. Jesus spoke about this, and encourages His own with these words:

At that time they will see the Son of Man coming in a cloud with power and great glory. When these things begin to take place, stand up and lift up your heads, because your redemption is drawing near. (Luke 21:27, 28)

Jesus will come in power and great glory riding on a white horse. The apostle John saw this majestic event in his vision: "I saw heaven standing open and there before me was a white horse, whose rider is called Faithful and True" (Rev. 19:11).

The heavenly armies will accompany Jesus: "The armies of heaven were following Him, riding on white horses" (Rev. 19:14). These armies will consist of a vast number of angels, as Jesus said in Matthew 25:31, where we read that He will come "in His glory, and all the holy angels with Him."

The great day will finally have come, and the Lord Jesus will return as King. The wonderful prophecy in Isaiah 33:17 will be fulfilled: "Your eyes will see the king in His beauty." Those who belong to Him will "be overjoyed when His glory is revealed" (1 Pet. 4:13).

Chapter 14

The Great Gathering

When Jesus returns, He will be accompanied by billions of angels. Before reaching earth, He is going to send some of them on a special mission:

> At that time men will see the Son of Man coming in clouds with great power and glory. And He will send His angels and gather His elect from the four winds, from the ends of the earth to the ends of the heavens. (Mark 13:26, 27)

These verses tell us the angels are going to gather Christ's elect when He is revealed in the clouds. According to what we have already seen, the elect are Christ's church.

We are informed the angels will gather the elect "from the ends of the earth to the ends of the heavens." To fully comprehend what this means, we can compare it to the parallel verse in Matthew 24. Verse 31 reads, "And He will send His angels with a great sound of a trumpet, and they will gather together His elect from the four winds, from one end of heaven to the other." Here, we are shown that Christ's angels will gather His elect from all over the earth and from all over heaven. This can be understood in the light of what Paul says in 1 Thessalonians 4, where he mentions two groups of people in connection with the return of Christ. One group comprises believers who are alive and remain and who shall be "caught up . . . in the clouds to meet the Lord in the air" (v.17). The other group Paul wrote about consists of those who are "dead in Christ" (v.16). They will be resurrected and gathered to Jesus along with the believers who are alive. These two groups comprise the elect who will be gathered by the angels. Hence, Christ's elect "from the ends of the earth" will be the believers on the earth who are alive at His coming; His elect "from one end of heaven to the other" are "the dead in Christ" who will be resurrected when He comes. They will be gathered from heaven because their spirits are now with Jesus in heaven. From Paul's words in 2 Corinthians 5:8 we can know that the spirits of the believers who have died are in heaven; he says that to be "away from the body" is to be "at home with the Lord."

When Jesus comes, the remains of the bodies of the believers who have died are going to be resurrected as glorious bodies. They will be reunited with their respective spirits who will be gathered from heaven. The believers who are alive will also receive a new body, as Paul explained:

> We eagerly await a Savior from there [heaven], the Lord Jesus Christ, who, by the power that enables Him to bring everything under His control, will transform our lowly bodies so that they will be like His glorious body. (Phil. 3:20, 21)

IN THE AIR SPACE

We have ascertained that when Jesus comes back all the believers will be gathered together to Him "in the clouds" (1 Thess. 4:17). This gathering will take place at a certain location. To find out where, let's look at what occurred when Jesus was taken up into heaven after His resurrection. Those who witnessed this event were His disciples. It is described in the Bible in the following way:

> He was taken up before their very eyes, and a cloud hid Him from their sight. They were looking intently up into the sky as He was going, when suddenly two men dressed in white stood beside them. 'Men of Galilee,' they said, 'why do you stand here looking into the sky? This same Jesus, who has been

taken from you into heaven, will come back *in the same way* you have seen Him go into heaven.' Then they returned to Jerusalem from the hill called the Mount of Olives, a Sabbath day's walk from the city. (Acts 1:9–12)

This passage informs us that Jesus ascended from a hill nearby Jerusalem called the Mount of Olives. Since Jesus will come back "in the same way" as He departed to heaven, we can expect Him to return to the exact place where He departed. Zechariah, one of the prophets of Israel, foretold that when Jesus returns He will descend on this very hill:

Then the Lord will go out and fight against those nations, as He fights in the day of battle. On that day His feet will stand on the Mount of Olives, east of Jerusalem. (Zech. 14:3, 4)

Before Jesus comes all the way down to the earth, He will gather the believers to Himself in the clouds. Therefore, we have every reason to believe that the gathering of the believers to Jesus will occur in the air space above Jerusalem. Here, there will be enough room for the many millions from the entire globe who will meet Jesus when He returns—and what a gathering it will be!

THE LORD'S ESCORT

The question now is what will become of all the believers after the great gathering. The last part of 1 Thessalonians 4:17 says the believers will be "caught up together . . . in the clouds to meet the Lord in the air. And so we will be with the Lord forever."

We can compare what Paul writes here to Christ's own teaching in Matthew 24, where He describes His second coming. The account ends with "His elect" being gathered by the angels when He appears in the clouds (v.31). As in Paul's description of the return of Christ in 1 Thessalonians 4, the end of the account hangs literally in the air. Only after several parables about His return, does Jesus tell us what will then take place. In Matthew 25:31–46 Jesus informs us that after His descent all the nations will be gathered before Him to be judged. This happens on the earth. And since we are told that when the gathering of the believers takes place they will then "be with the Lord" (1 Thess. 4:17), we can safely assume they will accompany Jesus in His descent to the earth after having met Him in the clouds.

This conclusion aligns with the meaning of *parousia*, the Greek term that is used for the "coming" of the Lord in 1 Thessalonians 4:15. The word *parousia* was a term used for a visit of the Caesar or a high-ranking official to a city. The rulers of the city went out to meet him and escort him back to the city on the final part of his journey. This seems to imply what will happen when Jesus returns; the believers from the whole world will "meet the Lord in the air" (1 Thess. 4:17) and then escort Him to the earth. The air space above Israel will therefore serve as the meeting place between Jesus and His church before their descent to Jerusalem.

MEETING THE LORD

Let's consider the Greek term *apántesis* ('meet') as used in 1 Thessalonians 4:17. We read here that the believers will "be caught up . . . in the clouds to meet [*apántesis*] the Lord in the air." The word *apántesis* is also used in Acts 28:15, where we read that believers from Rome went out to "meet" Paul. This verse provides us with an example of how this word was used at the time the New Testament was written. In the same way as Paul continued to Rome with the believers who came out from Rome to meet him, so will Jesus, when He comes, continue His descent to the earth with the believers who are caught up from the earth to meet Him in the air.

Another passage in the Bible where the word *apántesis* appears is in Matthew 25, where Jesus told the parable of the coming of the bridegroom. As was customary, a group of virgins (bridesmaids) "went out to meet [*apántesis*] the bridegroom" (v.1). They were to greet the bridegroom and escort him on the last leg of his journey to the house of the bride from where the virgins left to meet the bridegroom. This illustrates the sequence of events at the return of Jesus. In the same way as the bridegroom continues on his way to the house of the bride along with the virgins who came from her house to "meet [*apántesis*] him" (v.6), so will Jesus, when He comes, continue His descent to the earth with the believers who are caught up from the earth to meet Him in the air.

The above passages are the only places in the Bible where the word *apántesis* is used. There is, however, a variant of this word that also sheds light on events at the second coming of Jesus. That word is *hupántesis*. Its only occurrence is in John 12, where we read of Jesus coming to Jerusalem on a donkey. In verses 12 and 13 it says, "A great multitude that had come to the feast, when they heard that Jesus was coming to Jerusalem, took branches of palm trees and went out to meet [*hupántesis*] Him." This is indicative of what will transpire at the coming of Jesus in the future. In the same way as Jesus continued on to Jerusalem together with the great crowd who went out from Jerusalem to meet Him, so will Jesus, when He comes back, continue His descent to Jerusalem with the believers who are caught up from the earth to meet Him in the air.

Chapter 15

Christ versus Antichrist

When Jesus is revealed from heaven, He will put a sudden stop to the rampages of the Antichrist. He is going to crush the multinational forces that have overrun the land of Israel, and thereby save the Jews there from complete annihilation. The prophet Zechariah informs us that the Lord will fight against the armies that have taken Jerusalem and are in the process of devastating Israel:

> I will gather all the nations to Jerusalem to fight against it; the city will be captured, the houses ransacked, and the women raped. Half of the city will go into exile, but the rest of the people will not be taken from the city. Then the Lord will go out and fight against those nations, as He fights in the day of battle. (Zech. 14:2, 3)

The armies gathered against Jerusalem will be destroyed in a terrible way:

> This is the plague with which the Lord will strike all the nations that fought against Jerusalem: Their flesh will rot while they are still standing on their feet, their eyes will rot in their sockets, and their tongues will rot in their mouths. (Zech. 14:12)

What can make a person's skin, tongue, and eyes melt before

they even have time to fall to the ground? It could be the result of the intense heat that atomic bomb explosions generate during a nuclear war. The multinational forces are in fact going to attack each other:

> On that day men will be stricken by the Lord with great panic. Each man will seize the hand of another, and they will attack each other. (Zech. 14:13)

SPIRIT OUTPOURING AND SALVATION

The remaining Jews will experience the Spirit of God being poured out on them as Jesus is returning. The prophet Zechariah tells us:

> It shall be in that day that I will seek to destroy all the nations that come against Jerusalem. And I will pour on the house of David and the inhabitants of Jerusalem the Spirit of grace and supplication; then they will look on Me whom they pierced. Yes, they will mourn for Him as one mourns for his only son, and grieve for Him as one grieves for a firstborn. (Zech. 12:9, 10)

What a day it will be when the people of Israel realize that the crucified One whom they have rejected is their Messiah and Savior! The remaining remnant of Israel will experience a heartfelt revival, and they will grieve bitterly and mourn as someone who has lost their only child. On that day, the Jewish survivors will weep and repent of their sins and their rejection of Jesus. Then they will call on the name of the Lord:

> In the whole land, declares the Lord, two-thirds will be struck down and perish; yet one-third will be left in it. This third I will bring into the fire; I will refine them like silver and test them like gold. They will call on My name and I will answer them; I will say, 'They are My people,' and they will say, 'The Lord is our God.' (Zech. 13:8, 9)

The time of tribulation is now over for the people of Israel. They will experience divine deliverance:

> It will be a time of trouble for Jacob, but he will be saved out of it. In that day, declares the Lord Almighty, I will break the yoke off their necks and will tear off their bonds; no longer will foreigners enslave them. (Jer. 30:7, 8)

THE DEMISE OF THE ANTICHRIST

The book of Revelation gives us several details concerning the events that will take place the day Jesus returns:

> Then I saw the beast and the kings of the earth and their armies gathered together to make war against the rider on the horse and His army. But the beast was captured, and with him the false prophet who had performed the miraculous signs on his behalf. . . . The two of them were thrown alive into the fiery lake of burning sulfur. The rest of them were killed with the sword that came out of the mouth of the rider on the horse, and all the birds gorged themselves on their flesh. (Rev. 19:19–21)

In Daniel's book, the fate of the Antichrist is depicted several times. We read, "He will set up an abomination that causes desolation, until the end that is decreed is poured out on him" (Dan. 9:27); "He will destroy many and take his stand against the Prince of princes. Yet he will be destroyed, but not by human power" (Dan. 8:25); "The beast was slain and its body destroyed and thrown into the blazing fire" (Dan. 7:11). A last reference tells us where the Antichrist will be when Jesus returns:

> He will pitch his royal tents between the seas at the beautiful holy mountain. Yet he will come to his end, and no one will help him. (Dan. 11:45)

"The beautiful holy mountain" is Zion at Jerusalem, situated "between the seas" (the Mediterranean Sea and the Dead Sea).

Also Paul wrote about the fate of the Antichrist: "The lawless one will be revealed, whom the Lord will consume with the breath of His mouth and destroy with the brightness of His coming" (2 Thess. 2:8).

Paul informs us that when Jesus comes back to the earth He will not only punish the Antichrist, but also those who have rejected the gospel and persecuted the believers:

> God is just: He will pay back trouble to those who trouble you and give relief to you who are troubled, and to us as well. This will happen when the Lord Jesus is revealed from heaven in blazing fire with His powerful angels. He will punish those who do not know God and do not obey the gospel of our Lord Jesus. They will be punished with everlasting destruction and shut out from the presence of the Lord and from the majesty of His power on the day He comes to be glorified in His holy people and to be marveled at among all those who have believed. (2 Thess. 1:6–10)

The wrath of God will befall those who oppose God, and have embraced the Antichrist and received his mark (Rev. 14:9, 10). The prophet Isaiah described it this way:

> See, the Lord is coming with fire, and His chariots are like a whirlwind; He will bring down His anger with fury, and His rebuke with flames of fire. For with fire and with His sword the Lord will execute judgment upon all men, and many will be those slain by the Lord. (Is. 66:15, 16)

People who have not received the Antichrist's mark and who survive the outpouring of God's wrath will then have an opportunity to be under the kingship of Christ.

Chapter 16

The Coming Kingdom

King Nebuchadnezzar of ancient Babylon had a prophetic dream, in which he saw a great statue of a man. A stone fell and hit the statue on its toes, smashing them to pieces. The statue toppled over, was shattered, and the wind removed all traces of it. The stone that hit the statue became a great mountain, and filled the whole earth.

God gave the prophet Daniel the interpretation of the dream—and as we saw previously, the ten toes on the statue represent the ten rulers under the Antichrist:

> In the time of those kings, the God of heaven will set up a kingdom that will never be destroyed, nor will it be left to another people. It will crush all those kingdoms and bring them to an end, but it will itself endure forever. (Dan. 2:44)

There can be little doubt that the stone represents Jesus when He returns. In Luke 20:17 & 18, He says of Himself that He is the stone that grinds to powder whoever He falls on. He is going to crush the kingdom of the Antichrist and set up His own kingdom on the earth. Daniel relates:

> In my vision at night I looked, and there before me was one like a son of man, coming with the clouds of heaven. He approached the Ancient of Days and was led into His presence. He was given authority, glory and sovereign power; all peoples, nations and men of every language worshiped Him. His dominion is an everlasting dominion that will not pass away, and His kingdom is one that will never be destroyed. . . . Then the sovereignty, power and greatness of the kingdoms under the whole heaven will be handed over to the saints, the people of the Most High. His kingdom will be an everlasting kingdom, and all rulers will worship and obey Him. (Dan. 7:13, 14, 27)

Jesus Himself said, "When the Son of Man comes in His glory, and all the holy angels with Him, then He will sit on the throne of His glory" (Matt. 25:31). He will return to reign as "King of kings" (Rev. 19:16).

One of the first things to happen after Jesus has destroyed the kingdom of the Antichrist, will be the removal of the origin of all rebellion against God. This is described in the book of Revelation:

> And I saw an angel coming down out of heaven, having the key to the Abyss and holding in his hand a great chain. He seized the dragon, that ancient serpent, who is the devil, or Satan, and bound him for a thousand years. He threw him into the Abyss, and locked and sealed it over him, to keep him from deceiving the nations. (Rev. 20:1–3)

THE REWARD OF THE LORD

After Jesus has returned, the survivors among the nations will be gathered and judged by Him according to how they have treated His "brothers" (Matt. 25:31–46, cf. Matt. 12:50, where Jesus said, "Whoever does the will of My Father in heaven is My brother"). Those who have blessed Jesus' "brothers" will be cleansed and gain access to the kingdom (cf. Zeph. 3:9).

At this time, the appraisal of the believers will also take place. Paul writes:

> For we must all appear before the judgment seat of Christ, that each one may receive what is due him for the things done while in the body, whether good or bad. (2 Cor. 5:10)

We gain further insight into this in 1 Corinthians 3:13–15:

> Each one's work will be shown for what it is, because the Day will bring it to light. It will be revealed with fire, and the fire will test the quality of each man's work. If what he has built survives, he will receive his reward. If it is burned up, he will suffer loss; he himself will be saved, but only as one escaping through the flames.

The life and service of each believer will be appraised as to whether they are rewarded or not. Paul writes later in the same letter:

> Therefore judge nothing before the appointed time; wait till the Lord comes. He will bring to light what is hidden in darkness and will expose the motives of men's hearts. At that time each will receive his praise from God. (1 Cor. 4:5)

Jesus Himself says, "Behold, I am coming soon! My reward is with me, and I will give to everyone according to what he has done" (Rev. 22:12).

THE REIGN OF PEACE

The apostle Peter said that Jesus would remain in heaven "until the times of restoration of all things, which God has spoken by the mouth of all His holy prophets" (Acts 3:21). In connection with this, Peter made it clear that God will "send Jesus Christ" (Acts 3:20) so that "times of refreshing may come from the presence of the Lord" (Acts 3:19). The restoration of all things and the promised refreshment from the Lord will be made manifest in the coming kingdom.

When Jesus has come back, He will be personally present on the earth as King over all the nations (cf. Zech. 14:9). He is going to sit on His throne in Jerusalem, which will be the world capital (cf. Jer. 3:17).

The Bible says there will at last be peace on the earth when Jesus comes:

> He will judge between the nations and will settle disputes for many peoples. They will beat their swords into plowshares and their spears into pruning hooks. Nation will not take up sword against nation, nor will they train for war anymore. (Is. 2:4)

> The battle bow will be broken. He will proclaim peace to the nations. His rule will extend from sea to sea and from the River to the ends of the earth. (Zech. 9:10)

Jesus will reign over the nations with complete righteousness:

> Let the heavens rejoice, let the earth be glad; let the sea resound, and all that is in it; let the fields be jubilant, and everything in them. Then all the trees of the forest will sing for joy; they will sing before the Lord, for He comes, He comes to judge the earth. He will judge the world in righteousness and the peoples in His truth. (Ps. 96:11–13)

> May the nations be glad and sing for joy, for You rule the peoples justly and guide the nations of the earth. (Ps. 67:5)

Creation is going to be regenerated (Rom. 8:19–22), and according to Isaiah 11:6–9, there will be changes in wildlife. Predator instincts and the desire for meat will disappear from wild beasts. Their young and the offspring of tame animals will play together. Small children will be safe among animals that are mortally dangerous to approach at present. In addition, illness will decrease and people will attain very high ages (Is. 65:20).

The knowledge of the Lord will be global (Is. 11:19), and He is going to be worshipped by the whole world (Zech. 8:20–23). Zechariah 14:16 says, "And it shall come to pass that everyone who is left of all the nations which came against Jerusalem shall go up from year to year to worship the King, the LORD of hosts, and to keep the Feast of Tabernacles."

When Jesus exercises His power as King, the world will be a better place to live in:

> All kings will bow down to Him and all nations will serve Him.... Praise be to His glorious name forever; may the whole earth be filled with His glory. (Ps. 72:11, 19)

> The Lord reigns, let the earth be glad; let the distant shores rejoice. (Ps. 97:1)

THE GOVERNMENT IN THE KINGDOM

The world government in Christ's kingdom will consist of believers "from every tribe and language and people and nation" (Rev. 5:9). The next verse says they are "a kingdom and priests to serve our God, and they will reign on the earth."

Here are Christ's own words about His government in the coming kingdom:

> To him who overcomes and does My will to the end, I will give authority over the nations—He will rule them with an iron scepter; He will dash them to pieces like pottery'— just as I have received authority from My Father. (Rev. 2:26, 27)

Paul wrote about the future of the believers: "If we endure, we will also reign with Him" (2 Tim. 2:12). He also wrote, "The saints will [one day] judge and govern the world" (1 Cor. 6:2 AMP).

Concerning the people of Israel, the Bible informs us that Christ's first Jewish disciples will rule over them:

> Jesus said to them, 'Assuredly I say to you, that in the regeneration, when the Son of Man sits on the throne of His glory, you who have followed Me will also sit on twelve thrones, judging the twelve tribes of Israel.' (Matt. 19:28)

Judas, who was one of the twelve apostles, betrayed Jesus and thereby fell from his ministry (Acts 1:25). He was replaced by Matthias (v.26) in order that the apostles should be twelve in number. In this way, they will be able to occupy all twelve thrones and reign over the people of Israel in the coming kingdom.

A KINGDOM WITHIN THE KINGDOM

From the prophetic Scriptures, it is clear that the nation of Israel will have a special place within the worldwide kingdom that will be established when Jesus returns (cf. Is. 61:4–9). God is going to "restore the kingdom to Israel" (Acts 1:6). The borders of Israel's future kingdom are laid out in Ezekiel 47:13–21. Under the rulership of Jesus, the twelve tribes of Israel will inherit their respective areas in the Promised Land (cf. Ezek. 48:1–29).

The first thousand years of "the eternal kingdom of our Lord" (2 Pet. 1:11) appear to be a hyphen between the present condition of the earth and eternity (cf. Rev. 20:4–6). After the thousand years, Satan and his demons will receive their eternal judgment together with the unrighteous (cf. Rev. 20:10–15). Then "a new heaven and a new earth" will emerge (Rev. 21:1). In the beautiful holy city, the New Jerusalem that descends to the new earth (cf. Rev. 21:2), the redeemed will spend a blessed eternity in the wonderful presence of God (cf. Rev. 22:5).

Part 5

The Time is Drawing Near

Chapter 17

In Preparation

The situation in the world today is fast approaching the picture the biblical prophecies paint. Preconditions for the events of the great tribulation are being played out before our very eyes:

- False prophets and false messiahs are getting numerous.

- Wars and conflicts involve more and more nations.

- Epidemics affect people across the globe.

- Lawlessness is increasing.

- Hate toward believers is on the rise.

- Israel is in place as a state in the homeland of the Jews.

- Israel is in need of a peace treaty with her hostile neighbors.

- Anti-Zionism and anti-Semitism are widespread.

- Preparations are ongoing for the rebuilding of the temple in Jerusalem.

- Unrest in the Middle East is paving the way for the rise of the Antichrist.

- Constantly more countries have nuclear weapons.

The world is being staged for the great drama of the end time. Jesus said concerning the signs He told about prior to His return:

> When you see all these things, you know that it is near, right at the door. I tell you the truth, this generation will certainly not pass away until all these things have happened. (Matt. 24:33, 34)

By "this generation" Jesus appears to be referring to the final generation living in the time of His return. Moreover, when Jesus says "all these things" He is referring to the signs He told about that will reach their peak just prior to His revelation. The generation that lives and sees all these signs happening will be the last one.

Jesus seems to indicate that the end time signs will appear concurrently and they will increase in intensity. This is reflected in the situation at present and implies that we may well be living in the generation that will experience His return. If this is the case, then it is quite possible the Antichrist is alive today. We must wake up and be aware that the time from now until the coming of Christ can be shorter than we think.

LOOKING AHEAD

Our having knowledge of the future should lead to personal changes today. A bride to be who knows that her wedding day is only a few weeks away does not wait until the very last day before she prepares herself. Certainty of the coming day decides her plans and activities so that she is ready when the day finally arrives. God gave us knowledge of the future so that we can begin to prepare ourselves for it today.

Do you know Jesus? Have you received him into your life as Savior and Lord? If not, do it now! Turn from your sins and receive God's forgiveness. Only then can you make yourself ready for the return of Christ.

An integral part of being prepared is to always have an upward look. The Bible says we are to "eagerly wait for the

Savior, the Lord Jesus Christ (Phil. 3:20). The return of Christ is something we are to long for. The apostle Paul wrote of being among those "who have loved His appearing" (2 Tim. 4:8).

Another part of our preparation for the return of Christ is that we have an inward look. We must keep our hearts clean by confessing our wrongdoing and allowing the blood of Jesus to cleanse us from all unrighteousness (1 John 1:7–9). The apostle John also wrote:

> We know that when He appears, we shall be like Him, for we shall see Him as He is. Everyone who has this hope in Him purifies himself, just as He is pure. (1 John 3:2, 3)

The apostle Peter had the same thing in mind when he wrote: "So then, dear friends, since you are looking forward to this, make every effort to be found spotless, blameless and at peace with Him" (2 Pet. 3:14).

In addition to looking upwards and inwards, we must also have an outward look when we contemplate the return of Christ. We need to look beyond ourselves by serving the Lord. Jesus illustrated this in a parable:

> He said: A man of noble birth went to a distant country to have himself appointed king and then to return. So he called ten of his servants and gave them ten minas. 'Put this money to work,' he said, 'until I come back.' (Luke 19:12, 13)

Let us use what we have received of the Lord to serve Him, and may we do what we can to lead others to faith in Jesus. In this way, we "look forward to the day of God and speed its coming" (2 Pet. 3:12).

WATCHING AND WAITING

Another important part of our preparation is to be aware that in the end time deceivers bringing false teaching will multiply (Matt. 24:11). This should lead us to be watchful and on our guard:

> Therefore, dear friends, since you already know this, be on your guard so that you may not be carried away by the error of lawless men and fall from your secure position. But grow in the grace and knowledge of our Lord and Savior Jesus Christ. (2 Pet. 3:17, 18)

We must also be sober in mind and body, as Jesus said: "Be careful, or your hearts will be weighed down with dissipation, drunkenness and the anxieties of life, and that day will close on you unexpectedly like a trap" (Luke 21:34).

Above all, we must maintain a constant and prayerful relationship with Jesus. The disciple that was closest to Jesus while He was on the earth exhorts us to "continue in Him, so that when He appears we may be confident and unashamed before Him at His coming" (1 John 2:28).

In view of what will transpire in the end time, we have been given a powerful promise. God desires to strengthen our hearts in order to make us blameless and holy in view of the return of Christ. We see this in the following verses:

> May the Lord . . . strengthen your hearts so that you will be blameless and holy in the presence of our God and Father when our Lord Jesus comes with all His holy ones. (1 Thess. 3:12, 13)

> You eagerly wait for our Lord Jesus Christ to be revealed. He will keep you strong to the end, so that you will be blameless on the day of our Lord Jesus Christ. (1 Cor. 1:7, 8)

With this promise, we can meet the future with confidence.

Chapter 18

Overcoming in the Last Days

If we are really near the return of Christ we need to be vigilant so we won't be caught off guard when the great tribulation arrives. The Bible predicts the means that will be used against the church in the end time. They include heresy, false prophecy, deceiving signs, social boycott, as well as bloody persecution. These things are nothing new when it comes to tribulation the church has been exposed to throughout its history. The unique thing about the great tribulation is its scope and the degree to which it will affect the church.

Believers in Jesus are going to experience trials, suffering, imprisonment, and even death. Many believers in totalitarian countries are already facing all this. Under the Antichrist, these suppressive measures will be systematized. The common tribulation of the church will be expanded, and its intensity will increase in the end time just prior to the return of Christ. Persecution will no longer be limited to certain parts of the globe. Jesus said, "You will be hated by *all* nations because of me" (Matt. 24:9).

ENDURE TO THE END

In the last days, the church will not only suffer under the usual lawlessness in society; it will feel the world's contempt and hostility. The Antichrist will attempt to eliminate the church.

Only an intervention by God will end the time of tribulation and establish the dominion of God in the sight of all. This will happen when Jesus comes back. Until then, the believers must remain steadfast, maintain a faithful testimony, and defy every adversity and danger. Strength and courage will be given to the servants of God to preach the gospel in spite of severe persecution. Through the rigors of the end time, the faith of God's people will be refined:

> All kinds of trials . . . have come so that your faith—of greater worth than gold, which perishes even though refined by fire—may be proved genuine and may result in praise, glory and honor when Jesus Christ is revealed. (1 Pet. 1:6, 7)

Believers in the end time are called to resemble Shadrach, Meshach, and Abed-Nego who were exiled to Babylon. These men refused to bow down and worship the image King Nebuchadnezzar had erected. This resulted in them being thrown into the fiery furnace because they said to the king:

> Our God whom we serve is able to deliver us from the burning fiery furnace, and He will deliver us from your hand, O king. But if not, let it be known to you, O king, that we do not serve your gods, nor will we worship the gold image which you have set up. (Dan. 3:17, 18)

This should also be the attitude of believers when faced with the command to worship "the image of the beast" (Rev. 13:15). The three men in Babylon miraculously walked "in the midst of the fire" with a fourth man whose form was "like the Son of God" (Dan. 3:25). In the same way, the believers in the end time will experience that the Son of God will be present with His own in the great tribulation.

Jesus says to His church, "Do not fear any of those things which you are about to suffer. . . . prison . . . tribulation. . . . death" (Rev. 2:10). In Luke 12:4, He says, "My friends, do not be afraid of those who kill the body, and after that have no more they can do." Also, in Matthew 24, He says, "But he who endures to the end shall be saved" (v.13). Let's take to heart these exhortations. If we do not then we will be like "he who received the seed on stony places" in Christ's parable of the sower:

> He has no root in himself, but endures only for a while. For when tribulation or persecution arises because of the word, immediately he stumbles. (Matt. 13:20, 21)

SUFFERING FOR THE SAKE OF JESUS

The early church was aware of the reality of suffering and martyrdom. Jesus said to the apostles, "A time is coming when anyone who kills you will think he is offering a service to God" (John 16:2). In the Acts of the Apostles, we read of the stoning of Stephen, the first martyr in the church (Acts 7:59, 60), and the execution of James, the brother of John (Acts 12:2).

Leaders in the early church prepared their congregations for fiery trials they would have to go through. The apostle Peter, who ended his life on a cross, wrote to the believers, "Dear friends, do not be surprised at the painful trial you are suffering" (1 Pet. 4:12). Persecution continued under several Caesars of the Roman Empire and the believers suffered terribly. Throughout the centuries, many believers have suffered tribulation, and it continues to this day.

The idea that the church will not experience a time of tribulation before the return of Christ appeals to an escape-mentality in believers who shrink from suffering. This applies especially to believers in the West, who have little or no exposure to persecution and affliction, as believers in communist- or Muslim dominated countries are experiencing.

The Bible shows that to suffer for the sake of Jesus is a normal part of the life of a believer: "For to you it has been granted on behalf of Jesus, not only to believe in Him, but also to suffer for His sake" (Phil. 1:29). Paul also says, "We must through many tribulations enter the kingdom of God" (Acts 14:22). After being beaten, we find the apostles "rejoicing that they were counted worthy to suffer shame" for Christ's name

(Acts 5:41). Most of them died as martyrs, and in Peter's case Jesus showed him "by what death he would glorify God" (John 21:19).

Perhaps you are disturbed by the thought that the church will go through great tribulation, since you may have to suffer and perhaps even die for Christ's sake. But know this—millions of believers have been persecuted and become martyrs since the beginning of the church nearly two thousand years ago. If you have fear of being persecuted, let it fade in the light of Christ's soon return and the glory that shall be yours. Paul says:

> The Spirit Himself bears witness with our spirit that we are children of God, and if children, then heirs—heirs of God and joint heirs with Christ, if indeed we suffer with Him, that we may also be glorified together. For I consider that the sufferings of this present time are not worthy to be compared with the glory which shall be revealed in us. (Rom. 8:17, 18)

We also read, "For our light affliction, which is but for a moment, is working for us a far more exceeding and eternal weight of glory" (2 Cor. 4:17).

MORE THAN CONQUERORS

When it comes to being persecuted unto death, we must realize that the martyrs are those who have the victory, although their opponents seem to be the ones who triumph. We read in Revelation 13:7, "And it was granted to him [the Antichrist] to make war with the saints and to *overcome* them." However, we also read, "And they *overcame* him [the Devil and thereby the Antichrist] by the blood of the Lamb and by the word of their testimony, *and they did not love their lives to the death*" (Rev. 12:11). The martyred saints are also described as "those who have the victory over the beast [the Antichrist]" (Rev. 15:2). In line with this, Paul says the following:

> Who shall separate us from the love of Christ? Shall

tribulation, or distress, or persecution, or famine, or nakedness, or peril, or sword? As it is written: For Your sake we are killed all the day long; we are accounted as sheep for the slaughter. Yet in all these things we are *more than conquerors* through Him who loved us. (Rom. 8:35–37)

The apostle Peter gives us these exhortations:

To the degree that you share the sufferings of Christ, keep on rejoicing, so that also at the revelation of His glory you may rejoice with exultation. (1 Pet. 4:13)

Be sober, be vigilant; because your adversary the devil walks about like a roaring lion, seeking whom he may devour. Resist him, steadfast in the faith, knowing that the same sufferings are experienced by your brotherhood in the world. But may the God of all grace, who called us to His eternal glory by Christ Jesus, after you have suffered a while, perfect, establish, strengthen, and settle you. (1 Pet. 5:8–10)

Let us be totally surrendered to the Lord Jesus, and stay faithful to Him no matter what the cost may be. We do well to meditate on the following in view of the difficult time that lies ahead of the church:

Yea, though I walk through the valley of the shadow of death, I will fear no evil; For You are with me; Your rod and Your staff, they comfort me. (Ps. 23:4)

We must be firmly rooted in the faith. And as we move into the future, we need to be fully conscious of the reality behind these words of Jesus: "In the world you will have tribulation; but be of good cheer, I have overcome the world" (John 16:33).

Chapter 19

Staying Awake

After all we have looked at, a pressing question is: Can we know when Jesus will return? To arrive at the answer, we must notice what Jesus Himself says about the timing. In Matthew 24:36, He says, "No one knows about that day or hour, not even the angels in heaven, nor the Son, but only the Father."

Jesus says only the Father knows the exact time of His return. The date of this momentous event is a secret "the Father has set by His own authority" (Acts 1:7). Since we do not know the date of the return of Christ, He asks us to "keep watch" and be ready (Matt. 24:42, 44). To "keep watch" has to do with being spiritually alert, and staying awake morally speaking. When you are awake, then you are not sleeping, as Paul wrote:

> You are all sons of the light and sons of the day. We do not belong to the night or to the darkness. So then, let us not be like others, who are *asleep*, but let us *be alert* and self-controlled. (1 Thess. 5:5, 6)

To be "asleep" is to be spiritually and morally faithless. By staying awake and alert we can avoid this and be able to discern and be attentive.

SEEING AND KNOWING

Jesus says that end time believers should pay special attention to certain events. When these things happen then they will know that His return is near:

> Now learn this lesson from the fig tree: As soon as its twigs get tender and its leaves come out, you *know* that summer is near. Even so, *when you see all these things*, you *know* that it [Or 'He'] is near, right at the door. (Matt. 24:32, 33)

What are the believers supposed to see that heralds the return of Christ? One of the most prominent things will be "the abomination that causes desolation." Jesus said, *"When you see* standing in the holy place 'the abomination that causes desolation,' spoken of through the prophet Daniel" (Matt. 24:15). As we have already ascertained, this event will trigger the start of the "great tribulation" (v.21).

Jesus also mentioned false christs and false prophets who will "perform great signs and miracles" (v.24). Most notable among them will be the Antichrist and the false prophet who will perform "great signs" (Rev. 13:13). Then just before He comes back "the sun will be darkened, and the moon will not give its light; the stars will fall from the sky, and the heavenly bodies will be shaken" (v.29).

Not until we "see all these things," will we "know that He is near, right at the door." There are therefore distinct signs that will lead us from uncertainty about the time of the return of Christ to an awareness that it is just about to happen. This certainty will be attained when the time comes, and not before. To register all this we must stay awake and keep watch all the time. We are to keep watch precisely because we now do not know when the time will arrive, as Jesus said:

> Therefore keep watch, because you do not know on what day your Lord will come. (Matt. 24:42)

Jesus does not stop there, but continues to say:

> But understand this: If the owner of the house had known at what time of night the thief was coming, he would have kept

watch and would not have let his house be broken into. (Matt. 24:43)

Knowing when in the night the thief comes makes you watchful and prepared. This is the way it will be in the end time. To begin with, we keep watch to recognize the signs. Then comes the certainty that Christ's return is just around the corner: "Even so, when you *see* all these things, you *know* that it [or 'He'] is near, right at the door" (Matt. 24:33). When we are in the process of seeing "*all* these things," we will find ourselves in the great tribulation. Now the time will have come to keep watch, not because we do not know when Jesus will come, but because we now know. Jesus said that the owner of the house keeps watch when he knows at what time of night the thief will come. In this way, the return of Christ will not come unexpectedly as a thief we do not anticipate. Paul writes:

> You know very well that the day of the Lord will come like a thief in the night. . . . But you, brothers, are not in darkness so that this day should surprise you like a thief. (1 Thess. 5:2, 4)

Thus, it is not God's will for believers that the return of Christ should happen unexpectedly as a surprise. This is how the world will experience the day Christ returns, but if the believers keep awake, they will not be unprepared. Jesus says concerning this: "But if you do not wake up, I will come like a thief" (Rev. 3:3). This tells us that if we keep awake then Jesus will not come unexpectedly. He exhorts us to be careful so that the day of His return will not come like a trap:

> Be careful, or your hearts will be weighed down with dissipation, drunkenness and the anxieties of life, and that day will close on you unexpectedly like a trap. For it will come upon all those who live on the face of the whole earth. (Luke 21:34, 35)

FOREKNOWLEDGE

On one occasion, Jesus compared His return to the flood at the time of Noah:

> As it was in the days of Noah, so it will be at the coming of the Son of Man. For in the days before the flood, people were eating and drinking, marrying and giving in marriage, up to the day Noah entered the ark; and they knew nothing about what would happen until the flood came and took them all away. That is how it will be at the coming of the Son of Man. (Matt. 24:37–39)

The activities of the people at the time of Noah show they did not believe that a flood would come. They received therefore no knowledge of when the flood was due, but Noah did. One week before the deluge began God spoke to Noah:

> Seven days from now I will send rain on the earth for forty days and forty nights, and I will wipe from the face of the earth every living creature I have made. (Gen. 7:4)

As Noah received foreknowledge, so will watchful believers in the end time. They will, among other things, see and recognize "the abomination of desolation." Then they will know that three and a half years remain until Jesus comes back. Accordingly, Christ's return should not come unexpectedly upon the believers. What Paul says bears repeating: "But you, brothers, are not in darkness so that this day should surprise you like a thief" (1 Thess. 5:4).

When we look at what the Bible has to say about the return of Christ, we see that we cannot determine a date for this event. Only God the Father knows the exact day. Nevertheless, we do know that it will not happen tomorrow, or next week, or even next year, since the Antichrist has not yet arisen.

On the other hand, we cannot maintain with certainty that many years will pass before Jesus returns. To assert that there is still a long time left can become an excuse for careless living.

According to Jesus, the evil servant says, "'My master is taking a long time in coming,' and he then begins to beat the menservants and maidservants and to eat and drink and get drunk" (Luke 12:45). Rather, we are to resemble the wise servant who faithfully works for his master in the waiting time, irrespective of how long it may be. Jesus says:

> Who then is the faithful and wise manager, whom the master puts in charge of his servants to give them their food allowance at the proper time? It will be good for that servant whom the master finds doing so when he returns. I tell you the truth, he will put him in charge of all his possessions. (Luke 12:42–44)

By serving Jesus, we keep ourselves ready for His return. In this way, we will still be ready when the time comes.

SECTION 2

WHAT ABOUT THE RAPTURE?

Part 6

Theory and Reality

Chapter 20

A Question of Timing

One day when I was ten years old, I walked home from school as usual. Having arrived, I opened the door, but no one in my family was home! I rushed out into the garden at the back, but no one was there either. Suddenly I got panicky. I thought Jesus had come and fetched my family to heaven, and that I was left behind. It was terrible! And now the tribulation was about to begin. But then my mother came. She had been talking to the woman next door. You can imagine my relief!

What I envisioned that day was fortunately wrong. The reason I had these thoughts was because I believed Jesus could come at any moment in a secret way to fetch the church to heaven. This was due to having been exposed to a teaching that emphasized this view of the return of Christ.

The question we are going to take a deep look at in this section is whether it is reasonable to assume that Jesus will come and take the church out of the world before the great tribulation.

TRIBULATION AND THE RAPTURE

Tribulation has always been the plight of the church of God. Jesus said, "In the world you will have tribulation" (John 16:33). He sent this message to one of the seven churches in the book of Revelation: "I know of your . . . tribulation" (Rev. 2:9). Paul told believers: "We must through many tribulations enter the kingdom of God" (Acts 14:22). He experienced it himself: "Tribulations await me" (Acts 20:23). The early believers experienced their share of "persecutions and tribulations" (2 Thess. 1:4). Paul wrote to the believers and encouraged them to be "patient in tribulation" (Rom. 12:12). Moreover, in Revelation 1:9 we read, "I, John, both your brother and companion in tribulation."

Nevertheless, there are certain scholars who say we must differentiate between common tribulation and the great tribulation. It is asserted that even though the church experiences tribulation now, it will not be on the earth during the time of great tribulation. In addition to His return after the great tribulation, Jesus will also come before this time to fetch to heaven the believers who are ready. This is popularly called the rapture.

The term 'rapture' derives from the Latin *rapiemur*, meaning 'caught up.' This word appears in the Latin Vulgate translation of 1 Thessalonians 4:17, which says that when Jesus comes the believers will be "*caught up* together with them [the resurrected believers] in the clouds to meet the Lord in the air." What happens to the believers after being caught up to meet Jesus in the air is, however, strictly speaking beyond the meaning of the term 'rapture.' Whether the believers travel on to heaven together with Jesus, or accompany Him in His descent to the earth, depends on when the rapture happens in relation to the great tribulation.

It all boils down to whether believers in the end time should expect great tribulation, or not. Here, we must allow Scripture to speak for itself without approaching it with preconceived ideas. We should not construct a prophetic timetable and then place selected Bible references in that scheme. Rather, we should read objectively and submit to the Bible even when it nullifies our theories. Any theory we endorse needs to be questioned to see if it is viable or not.

THE WITNESS OF THE EARLY CHURCH

Before we examine in detail what the Bible says about the church and the great tribulation, let us take a glance at the past. Looking at the doctrine of the end time in the light of history, we discover that believers have always taught that the church will go through the time of great tribulation. The catching up of the believers to meet the Lord in the clouds has been understood to take place at the conclusion of the great tribulation when Jesus comes with power and great glory. This view can be traced back to the early church, and has been prominent throughout the centuries.

There are good examples of writings from the time of the early church to show that a relevant expectation of the coming of Christ can be coupled with the understanding that the great tribulation and the appearance of the Antichrist will precede Christ's return and the gathering of the saints. This line of thought is found in *Didache*, a piece of Christian instruction that was well known in the early church. It is dated as early as about 120 A.D., and was one of the most important handbooks that regulated the affairs of the church. The last part of the writing follows:

> Watch for your life's sake. Let not your lamps be quenched, nor your loins unloosed; but be ready, for you know not the hour in which our Lord will come. But come together often, seeking the things which are befitting to your souls: for the whole time of your faith will not profit you, if you are not made perfect in the last time. For in the last days false prophets and corrupters shall be multiplied, and the sheep shall be turned into wolves, and love shall be turned into hate; for when lawlessness increases, they shall hate and persecute and betray one another, and then shall appear the world-deceiver as Son of God, and shall do signs and wonders, and the earth shall be delivered into his hands, and he shall do iniquitous things which have never yet come to pass since the beginning. Then shall the creation of men come into the fire of trial, and many shall be made to stumble and shall perish; but those who endure in their faith shall be saved from under the curse itself. And then shall appear the signs of the truth: first, the sign of an outspreading in heaven, then the sign of the sound of the trumpet. And third, the resurrection of the dead—yet not of all, but as it is said: "The Lord shall come and all His saints with Him." Then shall the world see the Lord coming upon the clouds of heaven. (16:1–8)

This is a clear testimony that right from the beginning the

church believed that the gathering together of the resurrected and living believers to Jesus in the clouds would occur after the great tribulation.

The writings of Justin Martyr (110–165 A.D.) are another example of the early church's view of the return of Christ. From his *Dialogue with Trypho* we understand that Justin expected the church to go through the great tribulation and be persecuted by the Antichrist before the return of Christ:

> He shall come from heaven with glory, when the man of apostasy, who speaks strange things against the Most High, shall venture to do unlawful deeds on the earth against us the Christians. . . . Now it is evident that no one can terrify or subdue us who have believed in Jesus over all the world. For it is plain that, though beheaded, and crucified, and thrown to the wild beasts, and chains, and fire, and all other kinds of torture, we do not give up our confession; but the more such things happen, the more do others and in larger numbers become faithful, and worshippers of God through the name of Jesus. (chapter 110)

Justin, who became a martyr, felt that the sufferings to be inflicted by the Antichrist would be no worse than what believers were already suffering for Jesus.

Other church fathers from the first to the third century A.D. who wrote of the return of Christ include Irenaeus, Tertullian, Hippolytus, and Victorinus. Common to all of them is the conviction that the Antichrist will persecute the church in the great tribulation before Jesus returns. Here are excerpts from their writings:

> John, in the Apocalypse, indicated . . . what shall happen in the last times, and concerning the ten kings who shall then arise . . . They shall give their kingdom to the beast, and put the Church to flight. After that they shall be destroyed by the coming of our Lord. (Irenaeus, *Against Heresies*, book 5, chapter 26)

The beast Antichrist, with his false prophet will wage on the Church of God. (Tertullian, *On the Resurrection of the Flesh*, chapter 25)

The one thousand two hundred and three score days (the half of the week) during which the tyrant is to reign and persecute the Church, which flees from city to city, and seeks concealment in the wilderness among the mountains. (Hippolytus, *Treatise on Christ and Antichrist*, chapter 61)

The Lord, admonishing His churches concerning the last times and their dangers . . . three years and six months, in which with all his power the devil will avenge himself under Antichrist against the Church. (Victorinus, *Commentary on the Apocalypse*)

DARBYISM

It was not until the 1830's that a new doctrine arose. This teaching claimed that a chosen group of believers will be transferred to heaven before the time of the Antichrist, but that other believers will have to go through the great tribulation. John Darby (1800–1882), who was a member of the Brethren movement in England, became the most prominent spokesperson for this teaching. He vigorously promoted his views, first in his native country and later in America. Although warmly received by some, his teaching was rejected by other students of the Bible, or was first accepted and later rejected by others.

The new teaching spread slowly up to the beginning of the twentieth century when its popularity expanded rapidly. This was mainly due to the second edition of the Scofield Reference Bible that presented the theory as biblical doctrine. More than three million copies of this reference Bible were sold within fifty years of it first being published in 1917. In this way, millions of believers became exposed to this interpretation of the end time.

Many Bible schools began to propagate this way of interpreting the prophetic Scriptures, and many prophecy conferences made this teaching known. It is therefore no surprise that many Christian leaders in the last generation have assumed that the idea of the church being transferred to heaven before the great tribulation is a doctrine extending back to apostolic times. However, this popular theory has no support in the historical interpretation of the Bible.

Some expositors, however, think that Darby's teaching was rediscovered truth, but as we have noted, Christian writings from the early church do not confirm this.

Although the theory of a transfer of the church to heaven before the great tribulation seems to be widespread, many Bible expositors still believe that the church will meet Jesus in the air when He returns to the earth. These expositors have held on to the solid biblical and historical belief that the church will go through the great tribulation before Jesus returns.

A NEW CONVICTION

The first time I heard anyone teach about the rapture happening *after* the great tribulation was in 1984 when I was twenty-two years old. However, my upbringing with end time books, magazines, songs, movies, and preaching that portrayed the rapture happening *before* the great tribulation caused me to reject this 'new' teaching. Consequently, in the following years I attempted to gather material from the Bible in support of the rapture happening before the great tribulation.

One day in 1989 when I was in prayer, a clear conviction came over me that I was wrong about my conclusions! And when subsequently reading the Scriptures I began to see the prophetic passages in a new light. The biblical concept of the rapture happening after the great tribulation materialized. I discovered that the end time doctrine I grew up with did not line up with what the Bible actually says.

Chapter 21

Prophetic Scriptures and the End Time

The very first believers' understanding of the return of Christ was, of course, rooted in the teaching of Christ Himself. The apostles received Christ's teaching, and passed it on orally and by letter. The writings of the apostles were supplementary to what Jesus Himself had said about His coming, which according to Him, will occur after the great tribulation:

> But in those days, after that tribulation, the sun will be darkened, and the moon will not give its light; the stars of heaven will fall, and the powers in the heavens will be shaken. Then they will see the Son of Man coming in the clouds with great power and glory. (Mark 13:24–26)

The return of Christ was from the beginning portrayed as one great public event—Jesus will be revealed in glory, the believers will be gathered to Him, and God's kingdom will be set up on the earth. When the believers read the writings of the apostles, it was this portrayal of the return of Christ that was the basic teaching. They were also told about such things as the appearance of the Antichrist before Jesus returns, and the resurrection of the believers when He returns.

Peter and John were among the apostles who wrote about the

return of Christ (e.g. 1 Pet. 5:4; 2 Pet. 3:9; 1 John 3:2). Clearly, they had in mind what Jesus had taught them concerning His coming. These writings coincided with other writings that mentioned Christ's return by the apostle Paul, along with James (James 5:7) and Jude (Jude v.14). There were no discrepancies between any of these writings, and therefore no indication of a separate coming before the great tribulation.

With this in mind, we will now take a look at the second letter of Paul to the Thessalonians and the book of Revelation, which are central Scriptures concerning the end time. We shall see what they say about the church, the Antichrist, and the great tribulation.

2 THESSALONIANS AND THE END TIME

Paul wrote his second letter to the Thessalonians two or three years after he started the church in Thessalonica. Paul had been in the city just a few weeks before he was forced to leave those who had come to faith in Jesus during this time (Acts 17:1–10). Although Paul stayed there just a short while, it was necessary for him to tell the newly converted about "the man of sin," otherwise known as the Antichrist. Since the Antichrist will appear before the second coming of Christ, Paul made sure the church knew about this man. He wrote:

> Let no one deceive you by any means; for that Day will not come unless the falling away comes first, and the man of sin is revealed, the son of perdition, who opposes and exalts himself above all that is called God or that is worshiped, so that he sits as God in the temple of God, showing himself that he is God. *Do you not remember that when I was still with you I told you these things?* (2 Thess. 2:3–5)

The last sentence in this passage shows that Paul had spoken of the Antichrist during the weeks he was with the new believers in Thessalonica. It would be impractical of Paul to use time and energy on this if the church was going to be transferred to heaven before the appearance of the Antichrist. We have to ask ourselves—why would Paul go into detail about things that apparently did not concern the church when there were so many other things these new believers needed to receive teaching on? In fact, Paul was warning the church. He gave the believers details concerning the Antichrist so that they could recognize him when he appears:

> He sits as God in the temple of God, showing himself that he is God. . . . The coming of the lawless one is according to the working of Satan, with all power, signs, and lying wonders, and with all unrighteous deception among those who perish. . . . Therefore, brethren, stand fast. (2 Thess. 2:4, 9, 10, 15)

The reason Paul gave the church this information was that in his absence they had been tricked into believing that "the day of Christ had come," i.e. that it was upon them and therefore imminent. Paul corrected them by writing about what will take place beforehand:

> Now, brethren, concerning the coming of our Lord Jesus Christ and our gathering together to Him, we ask you, not to be soon shaken in mind or troubled, either by spirit or by word or by letter, as if from us, as though the day of Christ had come. Let no one deceive you by any means; for that Day will not come unless the falling away comes first, and the man of sin is revealed. (2 Thess. 2:1–3)

The Antichrist of the great tribulation is not irrelevant to the church. A warning is also given in 1 John 2:18: "You have heard that the Antichrist is coming." This statement certainly suggests that the church will be present when he appears. Moreover, since the Antichrist appears in connection with the great tribulation (Rev. 13:3–5), this means the church will be present at that time.

THE REVELATION AND THE END TIME

When it comes to the book of Revelation, we have to be aware that the apostle John addressed it to believers experiencing persecution. Most expositors date the book at the end of the first century when Caesar Domitian was persecuting the church. The author himself was in exile on the island of Patmos when he received his visions (1:9). The book of Revelation must therefore be respected as a book of consolation for persecuted believers, with final relevancy for those living just before the return of Christ.

It is apparent the whole concern of the book of Revelation is to prepare the Christian churches for tribulation and martyrdom. The purpose of the book is also to get believers ready for the return of Christ by awakening, exhorting, and comforting them, as well as encouraging them to endure until He comes.

The messages to the seven churches in chapters 2 and 3 all contain promises to "him who overcomes" (2:7, 11, 17, 26; 3:5, 12, 21). What it means to overcome here is made clear later in the book. In chapter 12, we read, "And they *overcame* him [Satan] by the blood of the Lamb and by the word of their testimony" (v.11). Then in chapter 15 John sees "those who have the victory over [i.e. overcome] the beast" (v.2). This suggests that believers in the churches who are given promises when they overcome are still on the earth when the events in the main portion of the book of Revelation take place.

A passage in chapter 13 also indicates that believers in the church are present in the great tribulation. It is introduced by this verse: "And all who dwell on the earth will worship him [the beast], whose names have not been written in the book of Life" (v.8). This means that the believers, "whose names are in the book of Life" (Phil. 4:3), are the ones who will not worship the Antichrist. As a result, they will be persecuted as the next verses in Revelation 13 show:

> If anyone has an ear, let him hear. He who leads into captivity shall go into captivity; he who kills with the sword must be killed with the sword. Here is the patience and the faith of *the saints*. (vv.9, 10)

Notice that also Paul calls the believers "the saints" about 40 times in his letters. In addition, we must be aware there isn't anything in Revelation 13 to suggest that all these people become believers after the great tribulation has begun.

What Christ says to the believers in Revelation 22:12 also shows that the great tribulation concerns the church: "And behold, I am coming quickly, and My reward is with Me, to give to every one according to his work." What can this be other than a reference to Christ's coming in chapter 19 after the great tribulation that is the only coming of Christ depicted in the book?

At the end of the book, Christ gives a stern warning and says, "I testify to everyone who hears the words of the prophecy of this book: If anyone adds to these things, God will add to him the plagues that are written in this book" (22:18). This means that by changing the Word of God one runs the risk of being subject to the plagues, which are clearly intended for those "who had the mark of the beast and those who worshiped his image" (16:2). From this, we can deduce that although the believers will be present in the great tribulation, it is the will of God to protect them from the plagues at this time.

In chapter 18 we read of a "voice from heaven saying, Come out of her [Babylon], *My people*, lest you receive of her plagues" (v.4). This also indicates that believers will be present in the great tribulation, but that it is not the will of God that any of them should be exposed to the plagues. The expression "My people" means the people of God. That this points to people in the church is evident from 1 Peter 2:10, which says that the believers "are now the *people* of God." Moreover, in 2 Corinthians 6:16, Paul conveys God's word to the believers: "I will be their God, and they shall be *My people*."

Verse 16 in the last chapter of the Revelation shows that the whole of the contents of the book is intended for the believers: "I, Jesus, have sent My angel to testify to you these things in the churches." It is explicitly stated here that the contents of the book, which mainly is a description of the great tribulation, concerns the believers. Therefore, the idea of the prophetic book of the New Testament not being addressed to the church, but to another group who live after the church is transferred to heaven, is unfeasible.

Chapter 22

Theories about the Return of Christ

In this chapter, we are going to look at some theories concerning the return of Christ that are prevalent today. We will consider them in the light of what the Bible says about the end time.

- *Isn't Christ going to come first in a hidden way to take the church to Himself, and then after a few years in a public way for the world?*

The Bible speaks only of Christ coming in a public way for both the church and the world at the same time. For example, the apostle John wrote to the churches:

> Behold, He is coming with clouds, and *every eye* will see Him, and they also who pierced Him. And all the tribes of the earth will mourn because of Him. (Rev. 1:7)

We do not read anywhere that Jesus is going to come first in a hidden way. Those who assert this have perhaps got such an idea from what Paul wrote in 1 Thessalonians 5:2: "You yourselves know perfectly that the day of the Lord so comes as a thief in the night." However, since Paul says *the day* of the Lord will come "as a thief in the night," the meaning is evidently not that Jesus should be likened to a thief who comes in a hidden way at night to take the church away. The comparison of the coming of the day of the Lord to "a thief in the night" emphasizes rather the unexpectedness of Christ's return.

We must also be aware that the day of the Lord coming "as a thief in the night" concerns those who are in darkness. Paul went on to say, "But you, brethren, are not in darkness, so that this Day should overtake you as a thief" (1 Thess. 5:4). Here, we see that those "in darkness" will experience the day of Christ's return as an unpleasant surprise, not those in the light because they await His public return.

To believe that Jesus is going to come in a hidden way several years before He comes publicly goes against the obvious meaning of the aforementioned passages in the Bible.

- *Isn't Christ going to come first to the atmospheric heaven as a bridegroom for His church, and then after a few years to the earth as king with His church?*

The coming of Christ as a bridegroom is based mainly on a parable in Matthew 25:1–13, where Jesus tells about His return. In this parable, He compares Himself to a bridegroom who is met by bridesmaids when He comes back.

To understand when this will take place, it is necessary to look at the context where the parable is found. In Matthew 24, Jesus tells about His kingly return in glory, visible to all, after the great tribulation (v.21, 30). What Jesus says here forms the backdrop for the parable in question in chapter 25. This shows us that what Jesus says in both Matthew 24 and 25 concerns the same return after the great tribulation. From this, we understand that Jesus is coming back in the capacity of both bridegroom and king at the same time.

According to the Bible, it is correct that Jesus is coming first to the atmospheric heaven for the church, and then to the earth with the church. However, to say there are several years in between is only speculation. We are informed that the church will meet Jesus in the air and accompany Him at His arrival (1 Thess. 4:17; 3:13). That these events are parts of one great act is brought out in 2 Thessalonians 1:7–10. We read here that when "the Lord Jesus is revealed from heaven," He will take "vengeance on those who do not know God." This is going to happen "when He comes, in that Day, to be glorified in His saints and to be admired among all who believe." It is apparent that on the day Jesus comes, He will be revealed to the church and simultaneously to the ungodly on the earth.

- *Aren't the believers the only ones who will see Jesus when He comes before the great tribulation, while everyone will see Him at His return after the great tribulation?*

The apostle John wrote, "We know that when He appears, we shall be like Him, for we shall *see Him* as He is" (1 John 3:2). Neither this verse, nor any other, says that only believers will see Jesus when He is revealed. John also wrote, "Behold, He is coming with clouds, and every eye will *see Him*. . . . And all the tribes of the earth will mourn because of Him" (Rev. 1:7). The revelation of Christ concerns everyone who has eyes to see with, both believers and unbelievers. Hence, there is no contradiction between believers seeing Jesus, and unbelievers seeing Him at His return, which He stated will occur only after the great tribulation (Matt. 24:29, 30, cf. v.21).

- *Won't the church age end before the great tribulation, when the believers are transferred to heaven?*

Jesus told His disciples, "Lo, I am with you always, even to the end of the age" (Matt. 28:20). In other words, Jesus said He would be with His church until "the end of the age." This phrase occurs also in Matthew 24:3, where the disciples asked Jesus, "What will be the sign of Your coming, and of *the end of the age?*" Christ's answer shows us that the end of the age will come when He returns after the great tribulation (vv.21, 30; 25:31). Putting all this together, we see that the end of the so-called 'church age' coincides with the end of the present age at the return of Christ after the great tribulation.

On the last day of this present age the resurrection of those who died as believers in Christ will take place. Jesus said, "And this is the will of Him who sent Me, that everyone who sees the Son and believes in Him may have everlasting life; and I will raise him up at *the last day*" (John 6:40). Paul informs us that this resurrection will occur at the return of Christ:

> For the Lord Himself will descend from heaven with a shout, with the voice of an archangel, and with the trumpet of God. *And the dead in Christ will rise first.* Then we who are alive and remain shall be caught up together with them in the clouds to meet the Lord in the air. (1 Thess. 4:16, 17)

This shows us that the believers will be caught up to "meet the Lord in the air" immediately after the resurrection on the last day of this present age.

From the above we deduct that the end of the present age, and hence the time of the church, will not arrive until Christ comes after the great tribulation.

- *Isn't the appraisal of the believers going to take place in heaven while the great tribulation is in progress on the earth?*

From what Jesus says, we understand that the appraisal of the believers will take place when He comes back in glory with the angels. In Matthew 16:27, He said, "For the Son of Man will come in the glory of His Father with His angels, and then He will *reward each according to his works*." This can be compared to what Jesus says in Revelation 22:12: "I am coming quickly, and My *reward* is with Me, to give to *every one according to his work.*" Jesus can only be referring here to His coming in glory with the angels in chapter 19 when He defeats the "beast" and the "false prophet" (vv.19, 20). This means that Christ's appraisal of the believers will occur after His takeover of the earth.

Paul refers to Christ judging the believers in 2 Corinthians 5:10: "For we must all appear before the judgment seat of Christ, that each one may receive the things done in the body, according to what he has done, whether good or bad." This is related to 1 Corinthians 3:13, where Paul writes, "Each one's work will become manifest; for the Day will declare it, because it will be *revealed* by *fire*." This refers to the return of Christ "when the Lord Jesus is *revealed* from heaven with His mighty angels, in flaming *fire*" (2 Thess. 1:7, 8).

The appraisal of the believers is seen therefore to take place on earth when Jesus has been revealed from heaven with His angels. Since this happens after the great tribulation, the believers are not appraised in heaven while the tribulation is in progress.

- *Isn't the rapture going to take place at an unforeseen time before the great tribulation?*

The rapture is described in 1 Thessalonians 4:17. We read here that the believers will be "caught up . . . in the clouds to meet the Lord in the air." This will happen at "the coming [Gk. *parousia*] of the Lord" (v.15). The Greek term *parousia* is also used in Matthew 24, where we read of "the coming [*parousia*] of the Son of Man" (v.27). We are told that this will occur "immediately after the tribulation of those days" (v.29), which refers to the period of "great tribulation" (v.21).

From this, we understand that the rapture of the believers will take place at Christ's *parousia*. We also see that Christ's *parousia* will take place after the great tribulation. Therefore, to insist that the rapture will take place before the great tribulation is the same as saying that there will be two *parousia* (one *parousia* before the great tribulation, and one afterwards). Such an idea is quite arbitrary. Only one *parousia* is presented in the Bible, which according to Jesus, will take place after the great

tribulation.

In 2 Thessalonians 2:1, Paul mentions "the coming [*parousia*] of our Lord Jesus Christ and our gathering together to Him [i.e. the rapture]." In verse 3, Paul explains that this cannot take place before the Antichrist appears: "That Day will not come unless the falling away comes first, and the man of sin is revealed." Paul says the Antichrist will be able to be identified because he, among other things, "opposes and exalts himself above all that is called God or that is worshiped" (2 Thess. 2:4). This happens at the time of the great tribulation (Rev. 13:4 ff).

Against this background, the believers are encouraged to be patient until the coming of Christ (2 Thess. 3:5; James 5:7, 8). Being patient means that some time can elapse before the coming of Christ occurs. That the waiting time will be characterized by tribulation is brought out by Paul's words about being "patient in tribulation" (Rom. 12:12).

Based on the above, we conclude that the rapture of the believers to meet Jesus when He comes will not occur at an unforeseen time before the great tribulation.

- *If the church is going to go through the great tribulation, then very many believers will be martyred. Wouldn't this mean that for the church the hope of the Lord's coming is not a hope of being glorified, but is reduced to a hope of resurrection?*

The concept of "hope" in the New Testament points to what will happen when Jesus returns. It is used in relation to the resurrection from the dead in Acts 2:26, 24:15, 26:6–8, and 1 Thessalonians 4:13. The word "hope" is related to receiving glory in Romans 5:2–5, and in Colossians 1:5 & 27. It occurs also in connection with final salvation in Romans 8:24 & 25, Galatians 5:5, 1 Thessalonians 5:8, Titus 1:2, 2:13, 3:7, and 1 Peter 1:13. All of these Scripture references tell us that the hope of the believers is everlasting glory, no matter if they are dead or alive. It can be summed up in the way the word "hope" is used in 1 John 3:3, where it has to do with becoming like Jesus when He comes (1 John 3:2). This concerns both believers who die before Jesus comes, as well as believers who are alive when He comes.

The apostle Paul writes about those "who are alive and *remain* until the coming of the Lord" (1 Thess. 4:15). He mentions them again in verse 17 ("who are alive and *remain*"). The Greek word that is translated "remain" means to "survive." It speaks about those believers who are survivors, and are glorified (1 Cor. 15:51, 52) and then caught up into the air to meet the Lord in the clouds when He comes (1 Thess. 4:17). That Paul is underlining that the believers who are alive when Jesus comes are survivors, tells us that just before Jesus comes there will be a time that is life-threatening to the believers. This is the great tribulation when very many believers will be martyred.

- *If the church, which is the bride of Christ, is going to go through the great tribulation, then she will be a battered bride. Isn't this an unbiblical view of the bride?*

In Revelation 19:7 & 8, we read about the bride of Christ: "'Let us be glad and rejoice and give Him [God] glory, for the marriage of the Lamb has come, and *His wife* has made herself ready.' And to her it was granted to be arrayed in fine linen, clean and bright, for the fine linen is the righteous acts of *the saints*." Here, we are informed that the bride of Christ consists of "the saints." The saints are mentioned throughout the book of Revelation, also in passages related to the great tribulation (Rev. 5:8; 8:3, 4; 11:18; 13:7, 10; 14:12; 15:3; 16:6; 17:6; 18:24; 20:9). This shows that people who make up the bride of Christ in chapter 19 will go through the great tribulation beforehand.

We should also note that what is said about the bride in chapter 19 takes place after the destruction of "the great harlot" (Rev. 19:2), which happens at the end of the tribulation (cf. Rev. 16:19). It is only after this event that all the saints are collectively clothed with wedding garments for "the marriage of the Lamb" (Rev. 19:7), which takes place at the return of Christ (cf. Rev. 19:11). The saints, both the resurrected and those who survive the tribulation, will then be revealed as the glorious bride of Christ.

Part 7

Under the Magnifying Glass

Chapter 23

Can Christ Return at Any Moment?

The teaching that claims Jesus will come and fetch the believers to heaven before the great tribulation, is based on certain Bible passages. We will take a closer look at these references in the following chapters.

To begin with, we will examine Christ's statements in Mark 13:32–36 and Revelation 16:15. Some interpreters use these references to show that Jesus can return at any moment, proving that Jesus will return before the great tribulation.

MARK 13:32–36

> But of that day and hour no one knows, neither the angels in heaven, nor the Son, but only the Father. Take heed, watch and pray; for you do not know when the time is. It is like a man going to a far country, who left his house and gave authority to his servants, and to each his work, and commanded the doorkeeper to watch. Watch therefore, for you do not know when the master of the house is coming—in the evening, at midnight, at the crowing of the rooster, or in the morning—lest, coming suddenly, he find you sleeping.

If we take these verses out of context, they can give the impression that the event described can happen at any moment. However, when Jesus said, *"that* day and hour," He was referring to His return that He mentioned earlier in His discourse: "Then they will see the Son of Man coming in clouds with great power and glory" (v.26). Jesus said emphatically that this will occur "after that tribulation" (v.24), which is a reference to the great tribulation, described in verse 19: "For in those days there will be tribulation, such as has not been from the beginning of creation which God created until this time, nor ever shall be."

Jesus said in verse 32 that even He did not know the "day and hour," but this does not mean that He can come at any moment. The reason for this is that He told of events concerning the great tribulation that will occur before He comes (Mark 13:14 ff). The final generation of believers will witness these events, as Jesus alludes to in verse 29: "When *you* see these things happening, know that it [the coming of Christ] is near, at the very doors." Here, Jesus is referring to, among other things, the sun being darkened, the moon not giving its light, and the heavenly bodies being shaken (vv.24, 25). He says all this will happen just after the great tribulation (v.24). Only then will it be possible to say that He is coming at any moment. Those who have been watching will no longer be ignorant of the nearness of the return of Christ.

In view of His return, Jesus exhorted His disciples to "watch" (Mark 13:35). This implies spiritual as well as moral alertness. Jesus says the believers are to "watch," not because He can come at any moment, but that they may always stay spiritually awake. When the time for Christ's coming arrives, those who are "watching" will still be spiritually awake. They will not be found "sleeping" (Mark 13:36), i.e. in a state of spiritual and moral unfaithfulness. According to Jesus, those in this state will experience His return as an unexpected surprise. We see this also in a parable in Luke 12, where Jesus tells of a servant who did not do according to his master's words: "The master of that servant will come on a day when he is not looking for him, and at an hour when he is not aware" (v.46).

Regarding the clause "in the evening, at midnight, at the crowing of the rooster, or in the morning" (Mark 13:35), we have to aware that these words relate to the parable Jesus had just told. This parable features a doorkeeper who is required to keep awake because he does not know exactly when in the four watches of the night his master will return home (Mark 13:33–37). Jesus is saying that His disciples are to keep awake all the time and not be found "sleeping" (v.36) when He comes. It is apparent that Jesus is speaking about being spiritually awake, i.e. not sleeping spiritually speaking. The apostle Paul conveys the same thought when he writes, "Therefore let us not sleep, as others do, but let us watch and be sober" (1 Thess. 5:6). Since the issue is spiritual sleep, this tells us that the different points in time from evening to morning in the parable when people usually sleep, mean something else than literal parts of the day. They can perhaps represent different times throughout history since the ascension of Christ, or different times in the life of a person who is living in the last generation. That it was not Christ's intention to say that He can come at any moment is plain to see in that He clearly said in Mark 13:24–27 that He is going to come after a time of tribulation that "has not been since the beginning of the creation which God created until this time, nor ever shall be" (v.19).

We are also told that the coming of Christ will happen "suddenly" (Mark 13:36), but neither does this mean that Jesus can come at any moment. We can compare what Jesus says here to a prophecy in Malachi 3:1, which concerns His return to Jerusalem: "And the Lord, whom you seek, will *suddenly come* to His temple." The Lord Jesus will "suddenly come" after the great tribulation.

The meaning of Mark 13:32–36 is evidently that although Christ will come after the great tribulation, the exact time of His coming is unknown to all except the Father. That Jesus is going to fetch the church to heaven before the great tribulation is not even hinted at in the end time discourse He held in Mark 13.

From what we have looked at, we conclude that Mark 13:32–36 does not prove that Jesus will come before the great tribulation.

REVELATION 16:15

The other reference we are going to look at is in the book Revelation, where Jesus says, "Behold, I am coming as a thief" (Rev. 16:15). It is thought by some that this means Jesus is going to come when least expected, i.e. at any moment before the great

tribulation.

Let's look at the context where we find these words of Jesus:

> And I saw three unclean spirits like frogs. . . . which go out to the kings of the earth and of the whole world, to gather them to the battle of that great day of God Almighty. *'Behold, I am coming as a thief.* Blessed is he who watches, and keeps his garments, lest he walk naked and they see his shame.' And they gathered them together to the place called in Hebrew, Armageddon. (Rev. 16:13–16)

We see here that in the midst of events at the end of the great tribulation Jesus announces He will come "as a thief." This expression cannot therefore mean that Jesus is going to come before the great tribulation. On the contrary, it means He will come suddenly and unexpectedly after the great tribulation. This is the way the unbelievers in the world will experience the return of Christ, as well as those believers who are not watchful. Jesus said in Revelation 3:3, "Therefore if you do not watch, I will come upon you as a thief."

However, believers who are watchful will not experience the return of Christ "as a thief" because Jesus continues in Revelation 16:15 to say, "Blessed is he who watches." Besides carrying the meaning of being spiritually alert, the command to "watch" also implies being able to interpret the signs of the times and be attentive to developments in the end time. This aligns with what Paul writes to the believers about the return of Christ: "But you, brethren, are not in darkness, so that this Day should overtake you as a thief. . . . Therefore . . . let us watch and be sober" (1 Thess. 5:4, 6). Paul also says, in conformity with Jesus, that the unbelievers will be those who will experience the day of the coming of the Lord as unexpectedly "as a thief in the night" (1 Thess. 5:2).

Summary: Mark 13:32–36 and Revelation 16:15 do not prove that Jesus can return at any moment. On the contrary, these references show that Jesus will return after the great tribulation.

Chapter 24

Will the Church Avoid the Tribulation?

Some expositors claim that what Jesus says in Luke 21:36 and Revelation 3:10 show that He is going to come and take the church to heaven before the great tribulation. Let's take a closer look at these references.

LUKE 21:36

> Watch therefore, and pray always that you may be counted worthy to escape all these things that will come to pass, and to stand before the Son of Man.

Notice Jesus says, "Watch therefore, and *pray always that you may be counted worthy* to escape all these things that will come to pass." This tells us it is those who pray to be counted worthy to escape all the things that are going to happen, who will receive an answer to prayer. Jesus is saying that those who do not pray to be counted worthy have no guarantee of escaping all the things that are going to happen. In other words, it is a question of being counted worthy, and this is dependent on praying about it. This suggests that what Jesus says here does not refer to a general transfer of believers to heaven before the great tribulation.

The words, "escape all *these things* that will come to pass" (v.36), must be viewed in the light of verse 31: "When you *see these things* happening, know that the kingdom of God is near."

Why does Jesus say to His followers they shall "*see* these things happening" (i.e. "all these things that will come to pass") if they are going to be transferred to heaven beforehand? Therefore, the context informs us that Jesus had something else in mind than a physical transfer out of the world before the great tribulation.

To find out what Jesus meant when He said, "escape all these things that will come to pass," we must look at what He said earlier in the chapter. In verse 12, we find the expression "all these things," as used in verse 36. This expression refers to, among other things, "wars and commotions" (v.9), "great earthquakes . . . famines and pestilences . . . fearful sights" (v.11). These are things the believers are to see (v.31) and pray to be counted worthy to escape so they can "stand before" Jesus when He comes "in a cloud with power and great glory" (v.27). We understand therefore, there will be believers on the earth in the end time who will avoid having to experience the awful things that will happen then. This is evident in several translations of Luke 21:36, among them Basic English: "But keep watch at all times with prayer, that you may be strong enough *to come through all these things* and take your place before the Son of man." Paul expressed it this way: "May your whole spirit, soul, and body be preserved blameless at the coming of our Lord Jesus Christ" (1 Thess. 5:23).

According to the above, I cannot see how Luke 21:36 can be used as an argument that the church will be transferred to heaven before the great tribulation. It is apparent that this verse is addressed to believers who will be present on the earth at that time. They are to pray to be able to evade all the catastrophes that will happen during the tribulation while they wait for Jesus to come back in power and great glory.

REVELATION 3:10

> Because you have kept My command to persevere, I also will keep you from the hour of trial which shall come upon the whole world, to test those who dwell on the earth.

From this verse, some assert that Jesus is giving a promise to come and take the church to heaven before the great tribulation. Let's therefore examine this verse to see if this is the case.

The phrase "keep [you] from" is *tereo ek* in Greek. We find this phrase also in a prayer of Jesus: "I do not pray that You should take them out of the world, but that You should *keep* [them] *from* the evil one" (John 17:15). Jesus did not pray that the disciples should be transferred bodily out of the world, but He did pray that God would preserve them from the evil one while they were in the world. This helps us to understand that the promise Jesus gives in Revelation 3:10 does not necessarily concern a bodily removal before the time of trial.

Notice that Jesus gives the promise because of a reason. He says, "Because you have *kept* My command to persevere." The Greek word for "kept" (*tereo*) is the same word translated "keep" in the same verse, where Jesus says, "I also will keep you from the hour of trial." The meaning of this verse is therefore: When "the hour of trial" comes, Jesus will keep those who have kept His command to persevere. Thus, Christ's words do not point to an evacuation before the great tribulation, but are a promise of emerging preserved from that time having persevered (cf. Rev. 14:12: "Here is the patience of the saints"). Therefore, what Jesus says in Revelation 3:10 does not tell us the church is in heaven during the great tribulation.

We can compare our deduction with what Paul wrote in 2 Timothy 3:11: ". . . what persecutions I endured. And out of them all the Lord delivered me." That the Lord delivered Paul out of all persecutions does not mean that he avoided experiencing them. On the contrary, Paul says that he "endured" persecutions.

We can also include here what Peter wrote to persecuted believers: "The Lord knows how to deliver the godly out of temptations [Gk. *peirasmos* – 'trials']." This verse tells of God's preservation of the godly in the midst of trials. In the same way, Revelation 3:10 conveys Christ's promise of preservation in "*the hour of* trial [Gk. *peirasmos*]." Moreover, this phrase can be compared with the phrase "*the hour of* His judgment" in Revelation 14:7. Both terms appear to refer not merely to the length of time the trial or judgment lasts, but to the actual trial or judgment itself. Jesus used the term "hour" in this way when He faced the cross and "prayed that if it were possible, *the hour* might pass from Him" (Mark 14:35). As Jesus emerged victorious from His "hour" of trial, so will believers who endure in the trial of the great tribulation in the end time.

The words of Jesus in Revelation 3:10 are a part of His message to the church in Philadelphia, one of the seven churches in Revelation 2 and 3. Jesus has this to say to the church in Smyrna, another one of the seven churches: "Do not fear any of those things which you are about to suffer. Indeed, the devil is about to throw some of you into prison, that you may be tested, and you will have tribulation ten days. Be faithful until death" (Rev. 2:10). Evidently, the church in Smyrna was not going to avoid tribulation and martyrdom.

The promise of being kept when "the hour of trial" comes is directed to just one of the seven churches. The number 'seven' was regarded as the perfect number by the peoples of antiquity because it represented wholeness. Therefore, when John wrote to seven churches, it can be assumed that what he wrote can be applied to the universal church. It seems that one part of the worldwide church, represented by the church in Philadelphia, will go through the time of tribulation intact. Another part of the universal church, represented by the church in Smyrna, will suffer martyrdom in the end time (cf. Rev. 17:6; 20:4).

This apparent disparity seems to be usual in Scripture. In Hebrews 11, we find a list of people whom God delivered, but then we read: "Others were tortured. . . . Still others had trial of mockings and scourgings, yes, and of chains and imprisonment. They were stoned, they were sawn in two . . . were slain with the sword" (vv.35–37). In addition, the book of Acts tells us that James was martyred (12:2), while Peter was freed from prison (12:6–10). Even today, there are churches in parts of the world that are going through severe suffering and lack freedom, while other churches are free and without suffering.

Summary: Luke 21:36 and Revelation 3:10 do not show that Jesus is going to come and take the church to heaven before the great tribulation. On the contrary, these references concern the preservation of believers on the earth in the great tribulation.

Chapter 25

Will Christ Fetch the Church to Heaven?

Many assert that John 14:2 & 3 and 1 Thessalonians 4:16 & 17 say the church will be fetched to heaven when Jesus comes. Let's look at these references and judge for ourselves.

JOHN 14:2 & 3

> In My Father's house are many mansions; if it were not so, I would have told you. I go to prepare a place for you. And if I go and prepare a place for you, I will come again and receive you to Myself; that where I am, there you may be also.

When examining this passage, we have to look at it in its context. On this occasion, Jesus was speaking to eleven of His disciples (Judas Iscariot had left them, John 13:30). It is a plain fact that these eleven men did not experience being fetched to heaven in their lifetime. Jesus predicted something else for them. Several days beforehand, He told them, "They will deliver you up to tribulation and kill you" (Matt. 24:9). All of them became martyrs except John who survived an attempt on his life. They were crucified, beheaded, stoned, or flogged to death. This is evident from the continuation of Christ's speech to the eleven: "The time is coming that whoever kills you will think that he offers God service" (John 16:2; cf. Peter's death in John 21:18 f).

Christ's first disciples were all going to die. What, then, did Jesus have in mind when He said to the eleven that He was going to "come again" and "receive" them to Himself?

To arrive at the answer, we must go back to what He introduced this statement with. He said, "I *go* to prepare a place for you" (John 14:2). Earlier the same evening Jesus had said, "The Son of Man indeed *goes* just as it is written of Him" (Mark 14:21). A little later, Jesus said to Peter, "Where I am *going* you cannot follow Me now, but you shall follow Me afterward" (John 13:36). We understand that Jesus spoke here of His death, "that He should *depart* from this world to the Father" (John 13:1).

Jesus said therefore that He would have to die to "prepare a place." How are we to comprehend the place Jesus went to prepare for the disciples? The Bible says that Jesus was "put to death in the flesh, but made alive by the Spirit" (1 Pet. 3:18). We read also that Jesus "has gone into heaven and is at the right hand of God" (v.22). He has "passed through the heavens" (Heb. 4:14), and has "entered . . . into heaven itself," and into the "true" tabernacle (Heb. 9:24). The earthly tabernacle or temple, which Jesus called "My Father's house" (John 2:16), was only a "shadow of the heavenly" (Heb. 8:5), where Jesus entered. Jesus has therefore gone into His Father's house in heaven, which is "the greater and more perfect tabernacle not made with hands" (Heb. 9:11). That Jesus said "In My Father's house" in John 14:2 underlines the fact that He had the heavenly tabernacle in mind when He said in verse 3, "I go to prepare a place for you."

Jesus went past the veil in the heavenly tabernacle (Heb. 6:19, 20), "to appear in the presence of God for us" (Heb. 9:24). He consecrated "a new and living way" (Heb. 10:20), which means that believers can "enter the Holiest by the blood of Jesus" (Heb. 10:19). The "Holiest," also called "the Most Holy *Place*" (Heb. 9:25), is apparently the "place" Jesus prepared by His death for His disciples.

Continuing, Jesus said to His disciples: "And if I go and prepare a place for you, I will *come again* and receive you to Myself" (v.3). How would Jesus "come again"? Let's see what Jesus Himself said. In verse 28, Jesus referred to what He said to the eleven about Him coming: "You have heard Me say to you, 'I am going away and *coming back to you*'" (v.28). This connects with what He said to them in verse 18: "I will not leave you orphans; I will *come to you*." Then in verse 23, Jesus said He would "come" and make His home with those who love Him. This was to happen by "the Holy Spirit, whom the Father will send in My name," He explained in verse 26. We see therefore that Jesus said four times in John 14 that He would come (v.3, 18, 23, and 28). It follows that what is in view here is Jesus coming to the disciples by His Spirit to receive them to Himself in close spiritual union. He expressed this in verse 20 as, "you in Me, and I in you." Several weeks later on the Day of Pentecost the disciples were filled with the Holy Spirit who is "the Spirit of Christ" (1 Pet. 1:11). Jesus did come back to the eleven disciples as He promised He would.

We now come to the last part of Christ's words to His disciples in John 14:3: "I will come again and receive you to Myself; that *where I am, there you may be also*." Christ's words here are a reiteration of a statement He made in chapter 12: "If anyone serves Me, let him follow Me; and *where I am, there* My servant will *be also*" (v.26). Jesus told His disciples where He is spiritually speaking. He said, "I am in the Father" (John 14:10). And after having spoken about the coming of the Spirit, He said, "At that day you will know that I am in My Father, and *you in Me*" (v.20). After the coming of the Spirit on the Day of Pentecost the disciples came, spiritually speaking, before the presence of God in the heavenly tabernacle Jesus had prepared for them. Jesus received the disciples to Himself so that they could be where He is, i.e. in the Father. Their lives were "hidden with Christ *in* God" (Col. 3:3), having been "raised up" and made to "sit together in the heavenly places in Christ Jesus" (Eph. 2:6).

Based on the above, Jesus could not have spoken about a bodily transfer to heaven in John 14:3. In the rest of the chapter, Jesus explained to the disciples what He had said, i.e. where He was to go, what He was to prepare, how He would come back to them, where He is spiritually speaking, and how they could be where He is. In other words, Jesus spoke in John 14:3 about His death, His high-priestly service in the heavenly tabernacle, and His Spirit's coming and work in the lives of the disciples, and thereby in every believer's life. Thus, John 14:3 has no bearing on whether the church will be fetched to heaven before the great

tribulation.

1 THESSALONIANS 4:16 & 17

> For the Lord Himself will descend from heaven with a shout, with the voice of an archangel, and with the trumpet of God. And the dead in Christ will rise first. Then we who are alive and remain shall be caught up together with them in the clouds to meet the Lord in the air. And thus we shall always be with the Lord.

Some expositors assert this passage says the believers will be fetched to heaven before the great tribulation. The reason for this is that the rapture is said to be part of a separate coming of Christ, which was revealed to Paul. However, we must be aware that Paul's description of the rapture begins with these words: "For this we say to you by the word of the Lord, that we who are alive and remain until the *coming* of the Lord" (1 Thess. 4:15). The Greek word for "coming" is *parousia*. We find this word also in Matthew 24:27, where we read of Christ's "coming" [*parousia*]. In verse 29, Jesus states that His coming will happen "immediately *after* the tribulation of those days," referring to the period of "great tribulation" in verse 21. While Paul says the rapture will occur at Christ's *parousia*, Jesus Himself says His *parousia* will take place after the great tribulation. This tells us the rapture will occur after the great tribulation.

Jesus uses the following words in His description of His return to the earth after the great tribulation: "clouds," "angels," "trumpet," and "gather together":

> All the tribes of the earth will mourn, and they will see the Son of Man coming on the *clouds* of heaven with power and great glory. And He will send His *angels* with a great sound of a *trumpet*, and they will *gather together* His elect. (Matt. 24:30, 31)

We find similar words in 1 Thessalonians 4:16 & 17. We read here of "*clouds*," "an *archangel*" signifying the presence of other angels (cf. 2 Thess. 1:7), and "the *trumpet* of God." The idea of being gathered together is apparent in that the resurrected and living believers "together . . . meet the Lord." Paul referred to this gathering to the Lord in 2 Thessalonians 2:1, where he wrote of "the coming of our Lord Jesus Christ and our *gathering together* to Him." This is another indication that Paul is reiterating what Jesus told concerning His coming after the great tribulation. Therefore, the rapture is not a part of a separate coming of Jesus disclosed to Paul. Rather, it is a more complete revelation of what Jesus spoke of when He said that His elect would be gathered when He comes in the clouds after the great tribulation. What Paul does is to specify that they will be "caught up . . . in the clouds to meet the Lord in the air."

When studying 1 Thessalonians 4:16 & 17, we see that Paul's main concern was to answer the church's question about what will happen to those who had died among them in view of Christ's return (v.13 ff). It was not necessary for Paul to give details here about everything else that will happen when Christ returns. These include the Antichrist's demise (2 Thess. 2:8), the destruction of all the wicked (2 Thess. 1:6–10), and the establishment of the kingdom (2 Tim. 4:1). The passage in question should not therefore be looked upon as an isolated event that will occur several years before Jesus returns to the earth to set up His kingdom.

In addition, we must be aware that Paul does not say in 1 Thessalonians 4 that Jesus will fetch the church to heaven. The word 'fetch' is not used here or elsewhere in the Bible in connection with the church at the return of Christ. What 1 Thessalonians 4 portrays is the believers being gathered to meet Jesus in the air when He descends to the earth to set up His kingdom.

Summary: John 14:2 & 3 and 1 Thessalonians 4:16 & 17 do not say that Christ will fetch the church to heaven. John 14:2 & 3 do not concern the return of Christ at all, but are about the work of the Spirit of Christ in the lives of the believers. Our study of 1 Thessalonians 4:16 & 17 shows that what is portrayed happens when Jesus returns to the earth after the great tribulation.

Chapter 26

God's Wrath and the Heavenly Elders

Two Scripture references that form a cornerstone of the doctrine of the church being transferred to heaven before the great tribulation are, 1 Thessalonians 1:10 and Revelation 4:4. Based on these verses many believe the church will be in heaven during the great tribulation. Let's take a look at these references in order to assess them.

1 THESSALONIANS 1:10

Paul writes here that we are to wait for God's Son from heaven "who delivers us from the wrath to come." From this statement, some expositors assert that Jesus will come and remove the church from the world before the great tribulation.

To find out what Paul actually meant by "the wrath to come" we must see if this expression is used elsewhere in the Bible. John the Baptist used it when he rebuked the Pharisees and the Sadducees. He said, "Brood of vipers! Who has warned you to flee from *the wrath to come*?" (Matt. 3:7). We can compare John's statement to what Jesus said to the scribes and the Pharisees: "Serpents, brood of vipers! How can you escape *the condemnation of hell*?" (Matt. 23:33). Evidently, the phrase "the wrath to come" is equivalent to "the condemnation of hell."

When Paul uses the word "wrath" it appears to have the same meaning as John the Baptist put into it. In Romans 5:9, Paul writes, "Having now been justified by His blood, we shall be saved from *wrath* through Him." Clearly, Paul was not writing to first century Christians in Rome about the great tribulation of the end time; he was referring to perdition that all the justified shall be saved from through Jesus. This is also the case in Romans 2:5, where Paul writes of all the unsaved in view of the day of judgment: "But in accordance with your hardness and your impenitent heart you are treasuring up for yourself *wrath* in the day of *wrath* and revelation of the righteous judgment of God." In these two references from his letter to the Romans, Paul is speaking about what all believers in all generations are saved from, and what awaits all the ungodly who have ever lived. What Paul writes cannot be limited to concern only people who are alive just before Jesus returns to the earth in power and glory.

That wrath has to do with the judgment of perdition is also seen in John 3:36, where eternal life is contrasted with God's wrath: "Whoever believes in the Son has *eternal life*, but whoever rejects the Son will not see life, for *God's wrath* remains on him." This can be compared to 1 Thessalonians 5:9: "For God did not appoint us to *wrath*, but to obtain *salvation* through our Lord Jesus Christ." Both of these verses show that the opposite of salvation is God's wrath, which again shows that "the wrath to come" that Jesus delivers us from is a reference to eternal perdition, and not a short time of tribulation on the earth.

According to the testimony of Scripture we have looked at, it cannot be asserted from 1 Thessalonians 1:10 that Jesus will come and transfer the believers to heaven before the great tribulation.

WRATH IN THE END TIME

While we are on the subject of the wrath of God, we can take a look at how wrath ties in with the end time. It is apparent from the book of Revelation that the wrath of God will come in full force when Jesus comes back to the earth. In chapter 6, we read about "the great day of His *wrath*" that comes after the sixth seal is opened (v.17). This day refers to the day Jesus returns, since the signs in the sun, the moon, and the stars, which occur in connection with the opening of the sixth seal (vv.12, 13), are identical to the signs Jesus says are going to occur "immediately after the tribulation of those days" (Matt. 24:29), and just before He comes (Matt. 24:29, 30; Luke 21:25–27).

The statement in Revelation 6:17—"For *the great day* of His wrath has come, and *who is able to stand?*" is an echo of Joel 2:11: "For *the day* of the Lord is *great* and very terrible; *who can endure it?*" That the day of the Lord's wrath refers to the day of the return of Christ is very evident if we compare these two verses with the following prophecy: "Behold, He is coming, says the Lord of hosts. But *who can endure the day* of His coming? And *who can stand* when He appears?" (Mal. 3:1, 2).

Furthermore, from Revelation 6:10 & 11 we understand that vengeance on those who kill believers will not be carried out until the number of those destined to be martyred is complete. This tells us the vengeance of God will not overtake the guilty before the last martyrs have been killed for Christ's sake. Therefore, the wrath of God will come when the time of martyrdom in the great tribulation has ended.

The great tribulation itself will be a time when people will feel the wrath of *Satan*: "Woe to the inhabitants of the earth and the sea! For the devil has come down to you, having great *wrath*, because he knows that he has a short time" (Rev. 12:12). This is evident, among other things, by the fact that he will "make war" with those "who keep the commandments of God and have the testimony of Jesus Christ" (Rev. 12:17). The wrath of God, however, will be manifested in the seven "bowls of the wrath of God" (Rev. 16:1). They are called the "last plagues" (Rev. 15:1), and will be poured out at the very end of the great tribulation. The wrath of God will not befall the believers because we read that it will specifically target those "who had the mark of the beast and those who worshiped his image" (Rev. 16:2).

When the seventh bowl of God's wrath is poured out, we read, "And great Babylon was remembered before God, to give her *the cup of the wine of the fierceness of His wrath*" (Rev. 16:19). The prediction of Revelation 14 will then be fulfilled:

> If anyone worships the beast and his image, and receives his

mark on his forehead or on his hand, he himself shall also drink of *the wine of the wrath of God*, which is poured out full strength into *the cup of His indignation.* . . .

So the angel thrust his sickle into the earth and gathered the vine of the earth, and threw it into *the great winepress of the wrath of God. And the winepress was trampled* outside the city, and the blood came out of the winepress, up to the horses' bridles, for one thousand six hundred furlongs. (Rev. 14:9, 10, 19, 20)

The context shows this will happen at the time of the return of Christ that we read about in chapter 19:

Then I saw heaven opened, and behold, a white horse. And He who sat on him was called Faithful and True, and in righteousness He judges and makes war. . . . *He Himself treads the winepress of the fierceness and wrath of Almighty God.* (vv.11, 15)

We read that the seven bowls of wrath are "the seven last plagues for in them the wrath of God is complete" (Rev. 15:1). This is followed by what Revelation 19:15 tells us about Jesus returning on His white horse and treading "the winepress of the fierceness and wrath of Almighty God." Since this shows that the wrath of God will be consummated when Jesus returns after the bowls, these bowls can be likened to the first drops of the coming wrath of God. When the seventh bowl is poured out, then the time for the return of Christ will have arrived, and the wrath of God will come in full force upon the earth.

In Revelation 11, the heavenly elders say to God, "Your wrath has come" (v.18). They say this in response to voices in heaven that proclaim, "The kingdom of the world has become the kingdom of our Lord and of His Christ, and He will reign for ever and ever" (v.15). Again, we see how God's wrath is connected to the return of Christ when the kingdom is set up.

CONDEMNATION OR SALVATION

Isaiah was a prophet who testified that the wrath of God will be fully revealed at the coming of Christ:

> For behold, the Lord will come with fire and with His chariots, like a whirlwind, to render His *anger with fury*, and His rebuke with *flames of fire*. For by fire and by His sword the Lord will judge all flesh. (Is. 66:15, 16)

We can compare this to Paul's description of Christ's return:

> The Lord Jesus [will be] revealed from heaven with His mighty angels, in *flaming fire* taking *vengeance* on those who do not know God. . . . These shall be punished with everlasting destruction from the presence of the Lord and from the glory of His power. (2 Thess. 1:7–9)

When the judgment of wrath overtakes the ungodly, the believers will be out of harm's way. Paul introduces the passage we just read in this way:

> God is just: He will pay back trouble to those who trouble you and give relief to you who are troubled, and to us as well. This will happen when the Lord Jesus is revealed from heaven with His mighty angels. (2 Thess. 1:6, 7)

The believers will avoid the revelation of God's wrath when Jesus returns by being gathered together to Him (1 Thess. 4:17). For them the return of Jesus will mean the completion of their salvation: "To those who eagerly wait for Him He will appear a second time . . . for salvation" (Heb. 9:28). However, for the ungodly it will mean wrathful judgment:

> Behold, the Lord comes with ten thousands of His saints, to execute judgment on all, to convict all who are ungodly

among them of all their ungodly deeds which they have committed in an ungodly way, and of all the harsh things which ungodly sinners have spoken against Him. (Jude vv.14, 15)

The preliminary stage of this judgment will be the bowls of wrath that are poured out on the wicked at the very end of the great tribulation. God's wrath will then come in full force at the revelation of Jesus when the believers are gathered to safety at His side.

REVELATION 4:4

The other Scripture reference we are going to look at that is used to assert the church will be in heaven during the great tribulation, is Revelation 4:4. Here we read:

Around the throne were twenty-four thrones, and on the thrones I saw twenty-four elders sitting, clothed in white robes; and they had crowns of gold on their heads.

Some expositors assert the twenty-four elders represent the church that Jesus will come and fetch to heaven before the great tribulation. The white robes the twenty-four elders wear are said to point to the resurrection of the saints at the coming of Christ. However, in Revelation 6:9–11, non-resurrected martyrs are given white robes to wear, thus annulling this theory.

These expositors also say the golden crowns the twenty-four elders wear are an indication that they are symbolic of all the believers who have been rewarded. This is because crowns are promised to the believers (1 Cor. 9:25; 2 Tim. 4:8; James 1:12; Rev. 2:10; Rev. 3:11). However, we must be aware that at the sounding of the seventh trumpet the twenty-four elders announce the forthcoming rewarding of the believers:

The twenty-four elders who sat before God on their thrones fell on their faces and worshiped God, saying: 'We give You thanks, O Lord God Almighty, the One who is and who was and who is to come, because You have taken Your great power and reigned. The nations were angry, and Your wrath has come, and the time of the dead, that they should be judged, and that *You should reward Your servants the prophets and the saints, and those who fear Your name, small and great.*' (Rev. 11:16–18)

Since the twenty-four crowned elders say this, they cannot be symbolic of all the believers who are going to be rewarded.

Those who claim that the elders signify the church in heaven point to chapter 5:9 & 10:

And they sang a new song, saying: 'You are worthy to take the scroll, and to open its seals; For You were slain, and have redeemed us to God by Your blood out of every tribe and tongue and people and nation, and have made us kings and priests to our God; and we shall reign on the earth.'

The wording of this song is used in support of the elders being the church. However, we need to consider the following points:

To begin with, not only the elders sing this song. Both "the four living creatures and the twenty-four elders" sing it (Rev. 5:8). Concerning the four living creatures, they show John the four horsemen (Rev. 6:1–7), and one of them "gave to the seven angels seven golden bowls" (Rev. 15:7). The four living creatures are apparently of heavenly origin, and are not redeemed to God from among people on the earth.

In addition, the older majority of Greek manuscripts show that the twenty-four elders and the four living creatures are singing in the third person. (The New King James Version cited above follows a late variant reading of the Greek text.) A more correct rendering of Revelation 5:9 & 10 is brought out in e.g. the English Standard Version: "By your blood you ransomed people for God from every tribe and language and people and nation, and you have made them a kingdom and priests to our God, and they shall reign on the earth." The twenty-four elders and the four living creatures are not singing about themselves, but of others who have been made "a kingdom and priests." John says of the believers in the church that Jesus has made them "kings and priests" (Rev. 1:6). This means the song is about the church that is going to reign on the earth.

In our assessment of who the twenty-four elders are, it must be noted that the word "elder" is used both in the Old- and New Testament, and designates a leader in God's covenant people, whether it is the people of Israel or the church. It is therefore natural to think of the number twenty-four in terms of "the *twelve* tribes of the children of Israel" (Rev. 21:12), and "the *twelve* apostles of the Lamb" (Rev. 21:14) who are associated with the New Testament church. The twenty-four elders can therefore be heavenly representatives of the people of God on the earth. They are evidently twenty-four individuals due to the fact that one of them converses with John (Rev. 7:13–17).

It is quite possible that the twenty-four elders in Revelation 4:4 are leaders of the priestly service in heaven. We find the background for this in 1 Chronicles 24, where King David divided the priests in Israel into twenty-four groups. He did this because of a revelation from God (1 Chron. 28:19). This suggests that the priestly service in the temple in Jerusalem was an earthly copy of ordinances in heaven. The twenty-four earthly "elders of the priests" (Jer. 19:1) could therefore have been patterned after twenty-four heavenly priestly elders. This thesis is supported by the fact that the elders have "golden bowls full of incense, which are the prayers of the saints" (Rev. 5:8). The saints pray from the earth and the elders in heaven carry their prayers to "the golden altar which was before the throne" so that they ascend before God (Rev. 8:3, 4). Evidently, the twenty-four heavenly elders have a priestly role.

Summary: 1 Thessalonians 1:10 and Revelation 4:4 do not prove that the church will be in heaven during the great tribulation. 1 Thessalonians 1:10 concerns being delivered from eternal perdition, not the end time tribulation. The group described in Revelation 4:4 is clearly not the church, but twenty-four individuals who have a priestly role in heaven.

Chapter 27

Will the Church See the Antichrist?

Some expositors say that two references in 2 Thessalonians 2 show that Jesus is going to come before the Antichrist appears. Let's take a closer look at the verses in question to investigate this interpretation.

2 THESSALONIANS 2:3

> Let no one deceive you by any means; for that Day will not come unless the falling away comes first, and the man of sin is revealed, the son of perdition.

Paul mentions here "the falling away" and the appearance of the Antichrist. Some say "the falling away" points to the departure of the church to heaven before the Antichrist appears. They say this is because according to the original Greek, the phrase, "falling away" means, "be removed" implying a departure. Admittedly, the verbal form of the Greek word carries the meaning of 'withdrawing' or 'removing' oneself from something or other. However, the verbal form is not used in 2 Thessalonians 2:3. Here, the noun is used.

To rightly understand what is meant by the "falling away" we must see if this phrase is used elsewhere in the Bible. The Greek term is *apostasia*, and appears just twice—in the verse in question and in Acts 21:21. In the reference in Acts, the word *apostasia* is in the verbal form, and is translated "forsake." In classic Greek, the noun of the word translated "forsake" is *apostasis*. This word means 'revolt' and is actually an older synonym of *apostasia*. Therefore, the use of the word *apostasia* in Acts 21:21 helps us to understand the meaning of its use as a noun in 2 Thessalonians 2:3. When Paul wrote of "the falling away," he appears to have had some sort of forsaking, revolt or rebellion in mind.

Strong's Greek Dictionary defines "the falling away" as 'defection from truth; apostasy' (cf. Gk. *apostasia*). Apostasy is rebellion against the truth. This has occurred all through history, but Paul wrote of "*the* falling away"—a significant revolt of a spiritual nature he also alludes to in 1 Timothy 4:1, where he says, "In latter times some will depart from the faith." In other words, there will be a discernible revolt against God in the end time that will pave the way for "the man of sin" (the Antichrist). Several Bible translations actually use the words "revolt" or "rebellion" to express *apostasia* (Barclay, English Standard Version, Good News, Jerusalem, Living, Moffatt, New English, New International Version, Way, Williams).

When Paul wrote of "the falling away" it is possible he was referring to what Jesus said in His end time discourse about a time that is coming when "many will *fall away*" (Matt. 24:10). The immediate context informs us this will come about due to hateful persecution (v.9), false prophets leading many astray (v.11), and lawlessness (v.12). Today, we see the contours of the final mass defection from the faith. Persecution of Christians is on the rise many places, false teaching is spreading, and lawlessness is increasing at an alarming rate. According to Jesus, "lawlessness will abound" in the end time (Matt. 24:12) and consequently "the lawless one," i.e. the Antichrist, will appear (2 Thess. 2:8).

Paul informs the church he is writing to that the day of the Lord "will not come unless the falling away comes first." We are told here that "the falling away" has to occur *before* the day of the Lord comes. Paul also implies that the gathering of the church to meet Jesus will happen *when* the day of the Lord comes (1 Thess. 4:15–5:2). This shows that "the falling away" happens before the coming of Christ and the gathering of the church.

The immediate context also rules out that "the falling away" is a removal of the church to heaven. This is because Paul says "the coming of our Lord Jesus Christ and our gathering together to Him" (2 Thess. 2:1) will not take place before "the falling away" happens (v.3). Paul would not be making any sense saying that Jesus must come and 'remove' the church to heaven before He comes and gathers the church.

The broader context also excludes any reference to a transfer of the church to heaven being the subject of 2 Thessalonians 2:3. We read in chapter 1:

> God [will] give you [the believers] who are troubled *rest* with us *when* the Lord Jesus is *revealed from heaven* with His mighty angels, in flaming fire taking vengeance on those who do not know God. (2 Thess. 1:6–8)

This passage is naturally related to chapter 2, verse 8, which says that Jesus will destroy the Antichrist "with the brightness of His coming." Since the believers will not be given "rest" until Jesus is "revealed from heaven," and since the Antichrist will be destroyed precisely when Jesus is revealed, it follows that the believers are still on earth at the time of the Antichrist.

2 THESSALONIANS 2:6 & 7

The second reference we shall look at from 2 Thessalonians 2, reads as follows:

> And now you know what is restraining, that he [the man of sin – v.3] may be revealed in his own time. For the mystery of lawlessness is already at work; only He who now restrains will do so until He is taken out of the way. (vv.6, 7)

Some assert that the church is "restraining" the Antichrist. From this it is assumed that the church will be "taken out of the way," i.e. transferred to heaven before the Antichrist appears. We will look at this opinion in the light of the following points:

To begin with, it is highly questionable to build such a decisive theory upon an obscure Scripture reference. A good rule when it comes to prophecy is to view obscure Scripture references in the light of clear ones. The basis has to be clear Scripture references, especially when it comes to future events.

Secondly, when Paul wrote to the church in Thessalonica about "He who now restrains," the context shows he was referring to something they knew about, but evidently it was not a direct reference to the church itself. The universal church, including the local church at Thessalonica, could not have been restraining the Antichrist because Paul was reminding the church that the Antichrist had not yet appeared, thus proving that "the day of Christ" had not yet come (2 Thess. 2:2, 3). Since Paul is saying that the Antichrist will be a sign for the believers, they cannot be transferred to heaven before he appears.

Thirdly, Paul would be contradicting himself if the church is restraining the Antichrist. He makes it clear that "the man of sin" will be revealed *before* Jesus comes (2 Thess. 2:2, 3) and will be destroyed *when* Jesus comes (v.8). Paul also makes it clear that the church will be gathered to Jesus *when* He comes (2 Thess. 2:1). Note that Paul gives no indication that Jesus will come back twice. The order of events will therefore be as follows:

1. "He" who is restraining is "taken out of the way."
2. The Antichrist appears.
3. The coming of Jesus and the gathering of the church to Him.
4. The Antichrist is destroyed by Jesus.

Consequently, the church will be present also after the restrainer is "taken out of the way."

Fourthly, the church cannot be restraining because the gender of the Greek term for church (*ekklesia*) is feminine, whereas the formulation of the phrase "He who now restrains" (*ho katechon*) is masculine.

We learn from Paul's letter to the believers in Thessalonica that they knew what was restraining the Antichrist. In 2 Thessalonians 2:6 we read, "And now you know what is restraining." We however, cannot be absolutely certain about what it is because we are simply not told. Personally though, I think there are several things that suggest it is the Holy Spirit. Let me explain:

In the original Greek text the word for 'spirit,' *pneuma*, is grammatically neuter, but is sometimes rendered as masculine (i.e. "He") when used of the Holy Spirit (e.g. John 16:13; 1 Peter 1:11). Therefore "what" is used in verse 6 ("you know *what* is restraining"), and "He" in verse 7 ("*He* who now restrains"). That the Holy Spirit restrains individuals is illustrated in Acts 16:7, where Paul, Silas, and Timothy were not permitted by the Holy Spirit to go into Bithynia.

The last part of 2 Thessalonians 2:7 reads, "He who now restrains will do so until He is taken out of the way." Some expositors assert that the phrase "taken out of the way" means 'to go to heaven,' and they say that since the church is indwelt by the Holy Spirit, the church must go to heaven together with the Holy Spirit before the Antichrist can be revealed. When assessing this idea we need to take a closer look at the expression "taken out of the way" in the original text. It literally says, 'comes from the midst.' The formulation in Greek implies separation or movement away from something. It can therefore be translated variously as: "is out of the way" (Contemporary English Version, English Standard Version, Jewish New Testament), "be out of the way" (Youngs Literal Translation), or "steps out of the way" (New Living Translation). This does not imply that the Holy Spirit is going to leave the earth, but that He will no longer restrain the Antichrist when the time comes for his appearance.

The Holy Spirit will not leave the earth before the appearance of the Antichrist because He will dwell in all the believers who are contemporary with the Antichrist. We are informed that at this time there will be people who "have the testimony [Gk. *marturia*] of Jesus Christ" (Rev. 12:17). In chapter 19, we are told what this is: "The testimony [Gk. *marturia*] of Jesus is the spirit of prophecy" (v.10), i.e. the Holy Spirit who gives gifts of prophecy (cf. 1 Cor. 12:9, 10). It is worth noting that the same John, who wrote Revelation, also wrote, "He who believes in the Son of God has the witness [Gk. *marturia*] in himself" (1 John 5:10). This is a reference to the Holy Spirit; "It is the Spirit who bears witness [Gk. *marturún*]" (v.6). From this, we see that the believers who are contemporary with the Antichrist have the Holy Spirit.

We conclude that 2 Thessalonians 2:6 & 7 do not imply that the Holy Spirit and the church will be transferred to heaven before the Antichrist is revealed. What is implied is that the Antichrist cannot be revealed before God allows it, "that he may be revealed in his own time" (2 Thess. 2:6). The Antichrist will be unable to 'step forward' until the Holy Spirit 'steps aside.'

Summary: 2 Thessalonians 2:3, 6 & 7 do not prove that Jesus is going to fetch the church to heaven before the appearance of the Antichrist. On the contrary, the context of these verses shows that the church will see the appearance of the Antichrist.

CONCLUSION

In the last few chapters, we have looked at several Scripture references that are used to promote the teaching of the church being transferred to heaven before the great tribulation. We have closely examined these references and have not found that any of them support such a view of the end time. We have seen that the wording and context of each Scripture reference goes against such an interpretation. The whole pre-tribulation theory is built on shaky ground since none of the references we have looked at can be used as proof of the church being taken to heaven before the great tribulation. It is self-evident that this theory is based on selected verses taken out of context.

Our study shows that the church will be caught up to meet Jesus in the air *after* the great tribulation. The timing will be when Jesus returns to set up His kingdom of universal peace on the earth. Thus, the rapture is not an evacuation of the believers to heaven before the great tribulation; rather, it refers to the gathering together of the believers to Jesus at His return to the earth. Without regard to how desirable it would be for the church to be in heaven during the great tribulation, all evidence shows that the church will be on the earth at this time.

In regards to what we have looked at, it is helpful to be aware that almost all of what Jesus taught about His return is found in Matthew 24 and 25. Other Scriptures where Jesus mentions His coming are either repeats or elaborations of what He said in these two chapters. Here, Jesus clearly says that He will come just after a short time of great tribulation, and then He tells parables to illustrate His coming. Nowhere in these two chapters does Jesus say or intimate that He will come before the time of tribulation.

It is also helpful to be aware that almost all of what the apostle Paul taught concerning Christ's return is in his two letters to the Thessalonians. His teaching spans two chapters in the first letter (1 Thess. 4:13–5:11) and two chapters in the second letter (2 Thess. 1:3–2:12). A thorough and systematic reading of these passages shows that Paul did not teach that Jesus will come both before and after the end time tribulation. He presents only one future coming of Jesus, at which time the believers are given rest from tribulation, and the Antichrist is destroyed. Thus, Paul reiterates the teaching of Jesus concerning His return that will happen after the great tribulation.

Part 8

The Last Stones Unturned

Answering More Arguments

In the previous part, we looked at certain verses that some expositors say show Jesus will come and fetch the church to heaven before the great tribulation. There are, however, additional references that are used. The arguments connected to these references are grouped in this part since they build on what we have already looked at. The references are arranged here in the order they appear in the Bible—from the Old Testament, the Gospels, the Letters, and the Book of Revelation. Besides the timing of the rapture, we also look at a few other general arguments concerning the great tribulation.

I answer all the arguments that follow in the light of the Bible's entire testimony of Christ's return. It is apparent that none of the scriptures that are referred to contain a clear statement of a transfer of the church to heaven before the great tribulation. The most that can be invoked for such a view are intimations and allegories, but this is not enough upon which to build a solid doctrine. The biblical evidence I present shows there will be only one future coming of Christ—after the great tribulation, when He will gather His people and reign on the earth.

From the Old Testament

"HE SHALL HIDE ME IN HIS PAVILION"

"For in the time of trouble He shall hide me in His pavilion; in the secret place of His tabernacle He shall hide me; He shall set me high upon a rock." (Ps. 27:5)

Isn't this a promise that the church will be fetched to heaven before the great tribulation?

Let's look at this verse in the light of the situation of David who wrote it. Apparently, he had enemies who wanted to kill him. They are mentioned both before and after the verse in question (vv.2, 6, 12). In this psalm, David puts his trust in the Lord that He will prevent him from being killed. That the Lord hides David in His "pavilion" has therefore nothing to do with being in heaven. On the contrary, it is an expression telling us that David relied on God to preserve him in a perilous situation. This is also the meaning of the Lord hiding him "in the secret place of His tabernacle." Similar expressions in Psalm 31:20 & 21, also written by David, underline this:

> Oh, how great is Your goodness, which You have laid up for those who fear you, which You have prepared for those who trust in You in the presence of the sons of men! *You shall hide them in the secret place of Your presence* from the plots of men! *You shall keep them secretly in a pavilion* from the strife of tongues.

We can readily see that this passage does not concern avoiding the great tribulation, but avoiding the plots of evil men.

David says the following in Psalm 40:2: "He also brought me up out of a horrible pit, out of the miry clay, and *set my feet upon a rock*, and established my steps." David uses imagery when he describes the Lord's help and protection. Therefore, when he writes that the Lord will set him "high upon a rock" in Psalm 27:5, neither should this be understood as a reference to the church being fetched to heaven before the great tribulation. Let's not read something into this verse that is not there.

"ENTER YOUR CHAMBERS"

"Your dead shall live. . . . Come, My people, enter your chambers, and shut your doors behind you; hide yourself, as it were, for a little moment, until the indignation is past. For behold, the Lord comes out of His place to punish the inhabitants of the earth for their iniquity." (Is. 26:19–21)

Isn't this a description of the resurrection at the rapture, the taking of the believers to heaven before the great tribulation, and then the second coming of Christ to the earth?

When the Lord said through Isaiah, "Your dead shall live," He was of course referring to what will happen to the believing dead when Christ returns and all the believers are gathered to meet Him in the air. In 1 Thessalonians 4, the apostle Paul alludes to the prophecy in Isaiah of the resurrection at the return of Christ: "For the Lord Himself will descend from heaven with a shout. . . . And the dead in Christ will rise first. Then we who are alive and remain shall be caught up together with them in the clouds to meet the Lord in the air" (v.16, 17).

When Paul wrote in this passage that Jesus will descend from heaven "with a shout," he was alluding to another prophecy of

Isaiah: "*The Lord shall go forth* like a mighty man; He shall stir up His zeal like a man of war. He shall cry out, yes, *shout* aloud; He shall prevail against His enemies" (Is. 42:13). We see here that when the Lord goes forth with a shout He will fight against His enemies. Paul is therefore referring to the Lord descending and being victorious over His enemies on the earth, which does not happen until after the great tribulation. This is supported by the fact that the phrase, "The Lord shall go forth" appears in a prophecy in Zechariah 14 about the return of Christ after the great tribulation: "Then *the Lord will go forth* and fight against those nations, as He fights in the day of battle. And in that day His feet will stand on the Mount of Olives."

From this we understand that the promise of the resurrection of the dead who died in the faith in Isaiah 26:19 ("Your dead shall live"), will be fulfilled at the coming of the Lord in verse 21, which says, "For behold, the Lord comes out of His place to punish the inhabitants of the earth for their iniquity." This is evidently the coming of Christ after the great tribulation.

When the Lord says in verse 20, "shut your doors behind you; hide yourself," He does not appear to be talking about shutting doors in heaven and going into hiding there because of things happening on the earth. There is, of course, no need to do that up there. Rather, He is giving instructions to His people on the earth about measures they need to take just before He returns. The scene is reminiscent of when the Israelites in Egypt were commanded to stay behind closed doors when God's wrath struck the Egyptians, killing all their firstborn (Ex. 12:22, 23). In a similar fashion, believers will need to seek shelter and hide themselves behind closed doors at the time immediately preceding Christ's return. This will be especially applicable at the outpouring of the fourth bowl of wrath when the sun is given power to scorch people with fire (Rev. 16:8).

It is evident that in the passage in question from Isaiah 26, the Lord is giving His people advance warning. He is telling them how to ensure protection for themselves in the very last days of the great tribulation before He returns and resurrects those in the faith. Therefore, this passage cannot be used to show that believers who have died will be resurrected and taken to heaven before the great tribulation.

"TAKEN AWAY FROM EVIL"

In Isaiah 57:1, it says, "The righteous is taken away from evil." Isn't this a promise that the church will be taken to heaven before the great tribulation?

In order to get a correct understanding of the quote from Isaiah 57:1, we need to look at the whole verse. The first part of the verse says, "The righteous *perishes*, and no man takes it to heart; merciful men are *taken away*, while no one considers." This is Hebrew poetry, where the same thought is expressed twice with different words. Apparently, to be "taken away" means to perish, or die. This is also evident in Job 32:22 that says, "I do not know how to flatter, else my Maker would soon *take* me *away*." That to be 'taken away' means to die can also be seen in Job 34:20: "In a moment they *die*, in the middle of the night; the people are shaken and pass away; the mighty are *taken away* without a hand." Isaiah 57:1 is therefore not a promise that the church will be taken to heaven before the great tribulation; it is speaking of righteous people who, when they breath their last, avoid evil that otherwise would have come upon them.

"THE TIME OF JACOB'S TROUBLE"

In Jeremiah 30:7, it says, "Alas! For that day is great, so that none is like it; and it is the time of Jacob's trouble, but he shall be saved out of it." This verse says that the time of trouble in the last days concerns "Jacob" who is the ancestor of the Jews. Doesn't this mean that the great tribulation concerns the Jews, and not the church, which in turn means that the church is not present, i.e. it has been removed to heaven before the great tribulation begins?

The prophecy of Jeremiah says that although the Jews will

experience a difficult period in the end time, they will be saved out of it. However, the fact that the great tribulation concerns the Jews, does not automatically mean that it doesn't concern anyone else. In Revelation 3:10, the great tribulation is called "the hour of trial which shall come upon *the whole world*, to test those who dwell on the earth." Here, we see that not only Jews will experience a difficult time. Then in Revelation 7:9, John sees "a great multitude which no one could number, of all nations, tribes, peoples, and tongues." In verse 14, John is told where these people come from: "These are the ones who come out of the great tribulation." Here too, we see that the great tribulation does not only concern the Jews. Believers from many different nations will endure the great tribulation. Paul said to believers in Christ's church, "We must through many tribulations enter the kingdom of God" (Acts 14:22). This tells us that also the church will have to endure tribulation before Jesus returns and sets up the kingdom of God. Consequently, Jeremiah 30:7 does not necessitate the removal of the church before the great tribulation.

"A COVENANT WITH MANY FOR ONE WEEK"

"Then he shall confirm a covenant with many for one week; but in the middle of the week he shall bring an end to sacrifice and offering. And on the wing of abominations shall be one who makes desolate, even until the consummation, which is determined, is poured out on the desolate." (Dan. 9:27)

The prophetic "week" mentioned here is the last of seventy "weeks." It is a time span of seven years encompassing the great tribulation and ending with the return of Christ to the earth. Since the prophecy concerns Israel, doesn't this mean that the church has to be taken to heaven before the final seven years?

To begin with, let's look at the whole prophecy of the

"weeks."

In the middle of the sixth century B.C., the angel Gabriel appeared to Daniel, one of the Jewish exiles in Babylon, and said:

> Seventy weeks are determined for your people and for your holy city, to finish the transgression, to make an end of sins, to make reconciliation for iniquity, to bring in everlasting righteousness, to seal up vision and prophecy, and to anoint the Most Holy. Know therefore and understand, that from the going forth of the command to restore and build Jerusalem until Messiah the Prince, there shall be seven weeks and sixty-two weeks; the street shall be built again, and the wall, even in troublesome times.
>
> And after the sixty-two weeks Messiah shall be cut off, but not for Himself; and the people of the prince who is to come shall destroy the city and the sanctuary. The end of it shall be with a flood, and till the end of the war desolations are determined. Then he shall confirm a covenant with many for one week; but in the middle of the week he shall bring an end to sacrifice and offering. And on the wing of abominations shall be one who makes desolate, even until the consummation, which is determined, is poured out on the desolate. (Dan. 9:24–27)

The angel Gabriel said the prophecy concerns Daniel's people, who are the Jews, and the holy city, which is Jerusalem. The "weeks," literally 'sevens,' are 'sevens' of years. A total of seventy 'sevens,' i.e. 490 years, are portrayed. When this time has passed, Israel's national chastisement will end, salvation will be bestowed, and the words of the prophets will all be fulfilled.

The total of seventy "weeks" is first divided into seven "weeks" or forty-nine years. This time began with the decree of the Persian king Artaxerxes I to rebuild Jerusalem that was issued in 445 B.C. (Neh. 2:1–8). The city was rebuilt during this initial period of forty-nine years. This is followed by the next division consisting of sixty-two "weeks" or 434 years. After this period, the "Messiah" would be "cut off." This happened when Christ was crucified in about 30 A.D.

Following the sixty-nine "weeks" there is a period of

indefinite length encompassing Israel's national rejection during which time Jerusalem and the temple would be destroyed (70 A.D.). Gentiles then occupy the city, and wars and desolations characterize the age.

The final "week" of seven years constitutes the climax of history before the establishment of the messianic kingdom. It is divided into two periods of three and a half years each. At the beginning of the first half, the Antichrist makes a covenant involving the Jews, who are restored in their land with a resumption of temple worship. In the middle of the "week" the Antichrist enters the temple, ceases the sacrifices of the Jews, and the time of the great tribulation ensues. The coming of Christ consummates this period of desolation, bringing righteousness to Israel and judgment upon the Antichrist.

The assertion of the church being transferred to heaven before the great tribulation is based on the presupposition that the church is a parenthesis within the frame of Daniel's prophecy. The time of the church is placed between the sixty-ninth and seventieth "week" in Daniel 9. The seventieth "week" is reserved for Jews only while the church is in heaven.

This teaching, however, is flawed because it is based on an argument from silence. It is only assumed that the church will be taken out of the world before the seventieth "week" begins. To allege this approach affects the way we view Christ's statements concerning the end time. This is because He told His disciples that the great tribulation will precede His return (cf. Matt. 24). If the church is going to be taken out of the world before the great tribulation, then Jesus could not have spoken of the church being on the earth in the time immediately prior to His coming. According to this way of thinking, it is asserted that Jesus spoke only of the Jews who would go through the great tribulation before He returns. Expositors who have this understanding of the teaching of Jesus admit that although His end time teaching does not concern the church, His ethical teaching is for the believers. This assertion contradicts the fact that the disciples, whom Jesus spoke to about the great tribulation in the end time, became leaders in the church after His resurrection (Mark 13:3 ff; Acts 12:1–3). This in turn means that the teaching of Jesus about the end time and the great tribulation concerns the church.

In Matthew 28:19 & 20, Jesus says, "Go therefore and make disciples of all nations, baptizing them in the name of the Father and of the Son and of the Holy Spirit, teaching them to observe *all things* that I have commanded you." These words concern the ministry of the church. The phrase "all things" includes Christ's instructions to His followers when He spoke to them about the great tribulation in the end time. The end time teaching of Jesus, as well as His ethical teaching, is therefore directed to the church. This implies the church will be present in the great tribulation that Jesus spoke about. The church cannot therefore be transferred to heaven before the last "week" in Daniel 9.

Daniel's prophecy of the "weeks" portrays the destruction of Jerusalem and the temple by the Romans in 70 A.D., about forty years after the beginning of the church in that very city. Daniel 9:26 says, "And the people of the prince who is to come shall destroy the city and the sanctuary." This tells us that the church is present in the fulfillment of the prophecy. There isn't anything in the continuation of the prophecy to suggest that the church is no longer on the earth when Jewish sacrifices are spoken of in the end time. The last two thousand years have shown that God has been dealing with both the Jews and the church simultaneously. God dispersed the Jews across the whole world with the church present. He has also preserved the identity of the Jews, and is now in the process of gathering them back to their own land as prophesied (Ezek. 37:21). It is plain to see that if God can deal with Israel as well as the church before the seventieth "week" begins, surely He can continue dealing with both after the start of the last "week." Since both the Jewish people and the church are involved in the end time, it is not a question of one or the other, but of both. The church and Israel have existed side by side ever since the beginning of the church, and there isn't anything to suggest that it will not continue like this right up to the return of Christ after the great tribulation.

The church is evidently not a parenthesis in the plan of God. It is His crowning work that will be complete when the Jewish people are saved at the return of Christ (cf. Rom. 11:25–27). Thus, we conclude that the prophecy in Daniel 9 does not necessitate the church being transferred to heaven before the great tribulation.

"HIDDEN IN THE DAY OF THE LORD'S ANGER"

In Zephaniah 2:3, it says, "It may be that you will be hidden in the day of the Lord's anger." Doesn't this mean that when the day of the Lord arrives the believers will be hidden in heaven?

Those who are addressed in this particular prophecy in Zephaniah are mentioned in the first half of the verse, which reads: "Seek the Lord, all you *meek* of the earth, who have upheld His justice. Seek righteousness, seek humility." This tells us those who can be hidden from the anger of the Lord on His day are the meek and humble. In the continuation of the prophecy about the day of the Lord's anger, the Lord says, "In that day . . . I will take away from your *midst* those who rejoice in your pride, and . . . I will leave in your *midst* a *meek* and humble people, and they shall trust in the name of the Lord" (Zeph. 3:11, 12). From this, we can deduct that those who are hidden when the day of the Lord arrives are protected by the Lord while still in the "midst" of other people who are on the earth. Thus, we cannot make Zephaniah 2:3 say something it does not.

From the Gospels

"THIS GOSPEL OF THE KINGDOM"

In Matthew 24:14, Christ says, "And this gospel of the kingdom will be preached in all the world as a witness to all the nations, and then the end will come." Didn't Christ have in mind the gospel of the coming kingdom that will be preached by Jews in the great tribulation, and not the gospel of grace that is presently being preached by the believers? Doesn't this imply that the church will be transferred to heaven before the great tribulation begins?

When we examine the Scriptures, we do not find any difference between "this gospel of the kingdom" and the gospel of grace. Paul said to the elders of the church in Ephesus that the ministry he received from the Lord was to "testify to *the gospel of the grace of God*" (Acts 20:24). In the next verse, he said he had been among them "preaching *the kingdom* of God" (Acts 20:25). Paul went on his missionary journeys "preaching *the kingdom* of God and teaching the things which concern the Lord Jesus Christ" (Acts 28:31).

Jesus said in Matthew 24:14, "This *gospel of the kingdom* will be preached in all the world as a witness *to all the nations*, and then *the end* will come." In Luke 24:47, He said, "Repentance and remission of sins should be preached in His name *to all nations.*" We see here that the gospel of the kingdom to all the nations involves the remission of sins, which implies God's grace. The church will continue to preach this gospel of grace "even to *the end* of the age" (Matt. 28:20), which will occur when Jesus comes after the great tribulation. There is no indication here that the church will be transferred to heaven beforehand and that Jews will then preach the coming kingdom in the tribulation.

"THE ABOMINATION OF DESOLATION"

When Christ talked about "the abomination of desolation" in Matthew 24:15 and the great tribulation that follows, wasn't He predicting the Roman siege of Jerusalem in the Jewish war of 66–70 A.D.? Doesn't this mean there will not be any period of great tribulation before Christ comes and raptures the church?

In Matthew 24:15, Jesus says that the prophet Daniel had spoken of "the abomination of desolation." We find a reference to this in Daniel 11:31, where "the abomination of desolation" is mentioned in connection with "forces" that "defile the sanctuary fortress" in Jerusalem. Many expositors claim this prophecy was fulfilled in 168 B.C. when the Syrian king, Antiochus Epiphanies, invaded the holy land, desecrated the temple (the sanctuary fortress), and killed tens of thousands of Jews. However, it is plain to see that Jesus sees the prophecy of Daniel as future, so the events of 168 B.C. were only foreshadows of what was still to come.

We can approach Christ's prediction of "the abomination of desolation" and the great tribulation in the same way. It was foreshadowed in the Jewish War when the Romans besieged and desolated Jerusalem, but awaits fulfillment in the future. When the time comes the Antichrist will perpetrate "the abomination of desolation," thereby triggering the great tribulation (Matt. 24:15, 16, 21, 22). The reason we can know this concerns the end time is that Jesus says He will come in glory in the clouds "immediately after" this period of great tribulation (vv.29, 30). Then His elect will be gathered (v.31), which is a reference to the rapture.

"ON THE SABBATH"

In Matthew 24:15, Christ mentions "the abomination of desolation." In this connection, He says, "Then let those who are in Judea flee to the mountains. . . . And pray that your flight may not be in winter or on the Sabbath" (vv.16, 20). Since the Sabbath is mentioned, doesn't this mean it is the Jews who are exhorted to pray to avoid having to flee on that day? Doesn't this imply that the church is not in the picture, and therefore already transferred to heaven when the flight to the mountains takes place?

When Jesus gave the warning to flee, it first applied to the believers who were in Judea in 66 A.D. At that time, the Romans under Cestius Gallus made an attack on Jerusalem. Then suddenly and unexpectedly, he pulled back his forces. At this maneuver, the believers left the city, as Jesus had told them to do. They fled to the mountains on the east side of the Jordan River. The Romans returned in 68 A.D., and Jerusalem fell in 70 A.D. The future fulfillment of Christ's words seems therefore to once again concern believers in biblical Judea when Jerusalem is taken by the Antichrist in the end time.

Concerning the Sabbath, it is probable that a flight on this day of rest would be easier for the enemy to discover than on any other day of the week. In addition, Christ's exhortation to pray that the flight not be on the Sabbath indicates that those who pray are aware of the time they are living in and what is going to happen. This cannot apply to unbelieving Jews who do not know or care what Jesus said. It must apply to believers who are in Israel. The mention of the Sabbath is therefore no proof that the church is in heaven at this time.

"AS THE LIGHTNING"

"For as the lightning comes from the east and flashes to

the west, so also will the coming of the Son of Man be. . . . Immediately after the tribulation of those days the sun will be darkened, and the moon will not give its light; the stars will fall from heaven, and the powers of the heavens will be shaken. Then the sign of the Son of Man will appear in heaven, and then all the tribes of the earth will mourn, and they will see the Son of Man coming on the clouds of heaven with power and great glory." (Matt. 24:27–30)

According to this passage, isn't Christ going to first come as quickly as lightning before the great tribulation to gather the church to Himself, and then come visibly for the world after the great tribulation?

This is a classic example of taking verses out of their context. By reading the verses prior to this passage, we see the whole picture. From verse 21 in Matthew 24, Jesus is describing what will happen in the period of "great tribulation" that He mentions in this verse. He says that during this time people will claim that "the Christ" (v.23) has already come discreetly, having appeared in a secret place "in the desert" or "in the inner rooms" (v.26). Jesus refutes this false assertion and tells His followers that they should not believe these people since His coming will be visible for everyone like the lightning (vv.27, 28). After this digression Jesus continues to speak about the cosmic signs that will occur after the great tribulation (v.29 ff), and that signal His coming.

Christ's words about His coming "as the lightning comes from the east and flashes to the west" (v.27), do not necessarily concern the speed of His coming, but only underline the fact that His coming will be visible to all. In this passage, Jesus is emphasizing that He will only come once—after the great tribulation. This is when the gathering of the church will take place, as seen in verse 31: "And He will send His angels with a great sound of a trumpet, and they will gather together His elect from the four winds, from one end of heaven to the other."

"THE ELECT"

Aren't "the elect" in Christ's end time discourse in Matthew 24, the Jewish people? Doesn't this mean the church will be in heaven during the great tribulation?

We find the expression "the elect" in verses 22 and 24 in Matthew 24, and then in verse 31 we encounter the phrase "His elect." The word "His" refers to "the Son of Man" (v.30), i.e. Christ. This tells us "the elect" are Christ's elect.

In Matthew 22:14, Jesus said to the Jews, "For many are called, but *few are chosen* [i.e. elected]." Romans 11:7 says, "What Israel sought so earnestly it did not obtain, but *the elect* did." We see here that only a small part of the people of Israel constitutes "the elect" or "chosen." Christ's elect cannot therefore depict the Jewish people as a whole.

In Mark's version of Christ's end time discourse, we also find the expression "the elect" (Mark 13:20). They are defined in the same verse as those "whom He [the Lord] has chosen." This aligns with Christ's words to His disciples in John 15:19: "I have *chosen* you out of the world." Jesus chose His disciples from the people of Israel and they became His elect. Since then, every Jew who becomes a believer in Jesus is reckoned among Christ's elect, and is one of the "chosen" (Rev. 17:14).

However, the elect include all believers in Jesus, both Jew and Gentile. Romans 1:16 says that the gospel of Christ "is the power of God to salvation for everyone who believes, for the Jew first and also for the Greek." We are told it was Jesus "who has made both one" (Eph. 2:14). The apostle Peter wrote to believers and called them "elect" (1 Pet. 1:2). In addition, the apostle Paul addressed believers as "the elect of God" (Col. 3:12). Therefore, when Jesus spoke of His elect in Matthew 24 He was referring to all the believers, who He collectively calls "My church" in Matthew 16:18. Accordingly, the elect of Christ are synonymous with the church of Christ.

Some may object to this by pointing out the fact that Matthew wrote his gospel for Jews, and thereby assert that "the elect" are only Jews. However, Christ's end time discourse in Matthew 24 is repeated with minor differences in Mark 13, where "the elect" are also mentioned (vv.20, 27). Since Mark wrote his gospel for Gentiles, this shows us "the elect" are comprised of both Jews and Gentiles united by faith in Christ.

A comparison between Matthew 24 and Matthew 10 also shows that Jesus spoke about His future disciples in His end time discourse. In Matthew 10, Jesus gives His disciples instructions regarding their ministry, and He also reveals how people, including family members, would treat them. In verses 21 and 22, He says: "Now brother will deliver up brother to death, and a father his child; and children will rise up against parents and cause them to be put to death. And you will be hated by all for My name's sake. But he who endures to the end will be saved." These words are virtually repeated in Matthew 24:9 & 13. We see therefore it is the followers of Jesus who were going to be hated by other family members. This also shows us that Jesus did not have the whole Jewish people in mind when He mentioned His elect in Matthew 24.

Concerning His elect, Jesus said the following: "If those days had not been cut short, no one would survive, but for the sake of *the elect* those days will be shortened" (Matt. 24:22). This verse states that the great tribulation will be short for the sake of Christ's elect—those who constitute His church. One cannot therefore argue from the excerpts about "the elect" in Matthew 24 that the church will be in heaven during the great tribulation.

"A GREAT SOUND OF A TRUMPET"

Concerning Christ's return, we read in Matthew 24:31, "And He will send His angels with a great sound of a trumpet, and they will gather together His elect from the four winds, from one end of heaven to the other." In Isaiah 27:13, we read, "So it shall be in that day that the great trumpet will be blown; they will come, who are about to perish in the land of Assyria, and they who are outcasts in the land of Egypt, and shall worship the Lord in the holy mount at Jerusalem." And in Isaiah 11:12, we read, "He will . . . assemble the outcasts of Israel, and gather together the dispersed of Judah from the four corners of the earth." These references in Isaiah are prophecies concerning the gathering of the Jews back to the land of Israel in the end time. Since Christ's words are similar to that of Isaiah the prophet, isn't He referring to the Jews, and not the church?

The above excerpts from the book of Isaiah are two of many prophecies concerning the final and complete gathering of the Jews back to the land of Israel when Jesus returns (e.g. Deut. 30:1–6; Ezek. 37:21, 22; 39:27, 28; Micah 2:12, 13; Zech. 8:7, 8). However, the church will also be gathered from the whole world when Jesus returns. Paul writes of "the coming of our Lord Jesus Christ and *our gathering together* to Him" (2 Thess. 2:1). Moreover, as the answer to the previous question shows, Christ's elect that are gathered when He comes as depicted in Matthew 24 are those who constitute His church.

As at the gathering of Israel, a trumpet will be sounded at the gathering of the church: "The Lord Himself will descend from heaven with a shout, with the voice of an archangel, and the *trumpet* of God. And the dead in Christ will rise first. Then we who are alive and remain shall be caught up together with them in the clouds to meet the Lord in the air" (1 Thess. 4:16, 17). This trumpet is called "the last trumpet" in 1 Corinthians 15: "We shall not all sleep, but we shall all be changed—in a moment, in the twinkling of an eye, at *the last trumpet*. For the trumpet will sound, and the dead will be raised incorruptible, and we shall be changed" (vv.51, 52). Since the gathering of the church occurs at "the last trumpet," this means the trumpet blast that signals the final gathering of Israel in the end time cannot come afterwards. This excludes the possibility of the gathering of the church occurring before the final gathering of Israel at Christ's return. Therefore, we are faced with two ways of looking at these trumpet blasts. They are either two different trumpet blasts, with the final gathering of Israel occurring before the gathering of the church, or else both coincide at the same trumpet blast. It is very probable that the last alternative is correct. When Jesus returns and the last trumpet is sounded, those who constitute His church will be gathered to Him in the air as He is descending to the land of Israel. Surviving, repentant Jews still dispersed, will then also be gathered to the land of Israel.

"THAT DAY OR HOUR"

In Matthew 24:36, Jesus says, "No one knows about that day or hour, not even the angels in heaven, nor the Son, but only the Father." Doesn't this mean that the return of Christ is imminent?

At first sight, this verse seems to show that no event need precede the coming of Christ. However, if we read the whole chapter containing Christ's end time discourse, we find there isn't anything to suggest this. Jesus does not give any indication that His coming is imminent. On the contrary, He says emphatically that He will come "immediately after" a time of great tribulation (Matt. 24:29 ff).

Although no one knows the day and hour, the believers should know the time-period of Christ's return. This is the whole point of Christ's parable of the fig tree in the same chapter. He shows that as the coming of summer has its signs so does His coming: "Now learn this parable from the fig tree: When its branch has already become tender and puts forth leaves, you *know* that summer is near. So you also, when you see all these things, *know* that it is near, at the very doors" (Matt. 24:32, 33). When the signs that Jesus told about in Matthew 24 occur, which include the outbreak of the great tribulation (v.21 ff), then it will be possible to know His coming is very near.

Besides the signs that Jesus gives, the Bible shows that certain other events must occur before the return of Christ, so that the believers should not expect Him at any time. In John 21:18 & 19, Jesus showed that Peter would be killed as an old man. Peter wrote later to the believers: "Shortly I must put off my tent, just as our Lord Jesus Christ showed me" (2 Pet. 1:14). This tells us the believers could not expect the return of Christ before Peter had become old and died as a martyr.

We are also told that the "coming of our Lord Jesus Christ and our gathering together to Him" (2 Thess. 2:1), cannot take place before "the man of sin" (the Antichrist) appears (v.3).

From the above, we see that certain events (both past and future) precede the coming of Jesus. His coming is therefore not imminent.

"AS THE DAYS OF NOAH WERE"

According to Matthew 24:37–39, won't life be going on as usual the very day Jesus returns? Doesn't this mean there will be no forewarning of His coming?

The passage in question reads as follows:

> But as the days of Noah were, so also will the coming of the Son of Man be. For as in the days before the flood, they were eating and drinking, marrying and giving in marriage, until the day that Noah entered the ark, and did not know until the flood came and took them all away, so also will the coming of the Son of Man be.

Jesus talks here of "the days of Noah" and says they were "the days before the flood." This was when Noah was building the ark in obedience to God. The people Noah lived among did not believe in what he said about the coming flood. Therefore, they carried on as usual—"eating and drinking, marrying and giving in marriage." All this showed they had no concern for what Noah was doing and saying. Their actions proved this. Jesus says they continued doing all this "until the day Noah entered the ark." Genesis 7 tells us that when the ark was finished, Noah and his family entered the ark with the animals, and then the flood came and drowned the ungodly. This reflects how it will be in the end time. Ungodly people will not believe in the coming judgment of God; they will carry on as usual until they are forced to face judgment when Jesus returns.

When judgment finally came at the time of Noah, the torrential rains put the world under water and the ark was lifted up. This illustrates what will happen when Jesus comes back. The saints will be lifted as the judgment comes as a flood at the return of Christ to the earth.

That Jesus will come after the end time tribulation is apparent from the context of His words in Matthew 24. He talked about Noah in conjunction with "the coming of the Son of Man" (vv.37, 39). Jesus was clearly pointing back to verse 30, where He told of "the Son of Man coming." The verse beforehand tells us when He will come: "Immediately after the tribulation of those days" (v.29).

Christ's reference to "the days of Noah" and the flood are also found in Luke 17:26 & 27. In the next verses, Jesus says:

> Likewise as it was also in the days of Lot: They ate, they drank, they bought, they sold, they planted, they built; but on the day that Lot went out of Sodom it rained fire and brimstone from heaven and destroyed them all. Even so will it be in the day when the Son of Man is revealed. (vv.28–30)

Jesus spoke here of "the days of Lot," which He likened to "the days of Noah" (v.26). Jesus said it was then people ate, drank, bought, sold, planted, and built. These activities were going on in "the days of Lot" *before* "the day that Lot went out of Sodom," which is likened to "the day when the Son of Man is revealed" with fiery judgment. However, on the very day Lot left Sodom and fire fell, the people were not going about their usual activities. Genesis 19:4 says, "The men of the city, the men of Sodom, both old and young, all the people from every quarter, surrounded the house." They wanted to molest the angels who had come to Lot's house, thinking they were mere men.

With this in mind, it is apparent Jesus is not saying people will be eating, drinking, buying, selling, planting and building on the very day He comes from heaven and is revealed. He was speaking of what was going on in the days of Lot before Sodom's final day came. That the sinful people of Sodom were going about their usual activity just shows they did not know or care about the coming judgment. Yet fire fell and consumed them the day Lot and his family escaped with the help of angels.

From the above we see that life will not be going on as usual the day Jesus returns. Moreover, since Jesus is going to come after the end time tribulation, His coming will not be without any forewarning.

"ONE WILL BE TAKEN AND THE OTHER LEFT"

In Matthew 24:40 & 41, we read about people who are "taken" and "left" when Jesus returns: "Two men will be in the field; one will be taken and the other left. Two women will be grinding with a hand mill; one will be taken and the other left." Doesn't being "taken" refer to being taken to heaven before the great tribulation, while being "left" refers to those who are left behind to face the time of tribulation?

To discern rightly the meaning of these two words we have to be aware of the context of what Jesus is saying. Earlier in the chapter, He told about the "great tribulation" (v.21). Then He told about His return "with power and great glory" in verse 30. When we read about being "taken" and "left" in verses 40 and 41, this tells us Jesus is referring to what will take place at His return, which He has just said will happen after the great tribulation.

We find the meaning of the words "taken" and "left" in Luke 17:33 & 34, where Jesus used these phrases with an introductory explanation. He said, "Whoever seeks to save his life will *lose it*, and whoever loses his life will *preserve it*. I tell you, in that night there will be two men in one bed: the one will be *taken* and the other will be *left*." From this, it is apparent that one of these phrases means to lose one's life, and the other means to preserve one's life in the sense of staying alive. Here in Luke 17 as well as in Matthew 24, Jesus connects the phrases He uses to the account of the flood in Genesis when most people lost their lives and only a few remained alive. In the verse just prior to the passage in Matthew 24 we are looking at, Jesus spoke of those who "did not know until the flood came and took them all away," and continued by saying, "So also will the coming of the Son of Man be" (Matt. 24:39; cf. Luke 17:26, 27). Jesus is comparing what happened at the flood at the time of Noah with what will happen when He comes after the great tribulation. It is in this context Jesus spoke of being "taken" and "left." This means those who were present at the time of the flood illustrate those who are "taken" and "left" at the return of Christ after the great tribulation. On the one side were the ungodly who lost their lives, and on the other, Noah and his family who remained alive.

The question is which term denotes which group. The answer can be derived from the continuation of Luke 17. In verses 34–36, Jesus said, "I tell you, in that night there will be two men in one bed: the one will be taken and the other will be left. Two women will be grinding together: the one will be taken and the other left. Two men will be in the field: the one will be taken and the other left." At this, the disciples asked Jesus a question. Verse 37 reads, "And they answered and said to Him, 'Where, Lord?'" The disciples evidently asked Jesus about those who are "taken" because they were obviously not asking about the ones who were "left" in the bed, at the grinding mill, and in the field. Notice the answer Jesus gave: "Wherever the body is, there the eagles will be gathered together." This is the same as what Jesus says in Matthew 24:28: "For wherever the carcass is, there the eagles will be gathered together." (The Greek word translated "eagles" is rendered "vultures" in many translations since it includes vultures in the animal class of eagles.) Here, Jesus may very well be referring to Proverbs 30:17, which speaks of birds of prey that eat the corpses of the ungodly. Thus, we see that being "taken" is directly related to the mention of a dead body attracting birds of prey. In other words, it speaks of losing one's life.

The word "taken" is *paralambano* in Greek. Let's look at some examples of how this word is used in the book of Matthew: "When he [Joseph] arose, he *took* the young Child and His mother by night and departed for Egypt" (2:14); "Then the devil *took* Him [Jesus] up into the holy city" (4:5); "Then he [the unclean spirit] goes and *takes* with him seven other spirits more wicked than himself, and they enter and dwell there" (12:45); "Now Jesus, going up to Jerusalem, *took* the twelve disciples aside on the road" (20:17); "Then the soldiers of the governor *took* Jesus into the Praetorium" (27:27). These examples tell us the word *paralambano* is used in the sense of escorting, whether it be Jesus, Joseph, an unclean spirit, the devil, or soldiers who do it. Since the use of the word *paralambano* includes unpleasant circumstances, Jesus seems to comparing those who will be "taken" in Matthew 24:40 with those whom "the flood came and *took*" (v.39). Apparently, the ungodly in the end time will be escorted away and perish at the return of Christ. The taking of the ungodly at this time appears to be the subject of what Jesus says in Matthew 13, where He states concerning "the end of this age" (v.40): "The Son of Man will send out His angels, and they will gather out of His kingdom all things that offend, and those who practice lawlessness" (v.41). Thus, at the return of Christ, the ungodly will be "taken" by Christ's angels, and they will lose their lives.

Since the word "taken" has a negative connotation, then the word "left" would denote something positive. When Jesus in Matthew 24 uses Noah and his family to illustrate those who will remain alive when judgment comes at His return, it is worth noticing that in the flood account in Genesis 7, it says in verse 23, "Only Noah was *left*, together with those that were with him in the ark." Noah and his family were those who remained alive at the time of the flood, and this shows that the word "left" as used in this setting is a positive term. We should also note that Jesus did not say 'left behind,' which conjures up a different meaning altogether.

That being "taken" means to lose one's life, and being "left" means to preserve one's life, is also apparent when we look at the sentence structure in Luke 17:33 & 34: "Whoever seeks to save his life *will lose it* [A], and whoever loses his life *will preserve it* [B]. I tell you, in that night there will be two men in one bed: the one *will be taken* [A] and the other *will be left* [B]."

An end time prophecy in Zephaniah can also help us see the meaning of being "taken" and "left." In chapter 3, verses 11 and

12, we read, "In that day . . . I will *take* away from your midst those who rejoice in your pride . . . . I will *leave* in your midst a meek and humble people." Again, we see indications that to be "taken" is a negative thing, and to be "left" is a positive thing.

Based on the above, we see that the terms "taken" and "left" that Jesus used do not imply that He is going to come before the great tribulation. He spoke of those who lose their lives and those who remain alive when He comes after the great tribulation. Among those who remain alive will be the believers who will then be caught up to meet the Lord in the air (cf. 1 Thess. 4:17). Apparently, also many non-believers who have not received the mark of the beast (cf. Rev. 14:9, 10) will remain alive when Jesus comes back.

"COMING AT A HOUR YOU DO NOT EXPECT"

In Matthew 24:44, Jesus said, "Therefore you also be ready, for the Son of Man is coming at an hour you do not expect." Doesn't this mean Jesus can come at any moment?

Jesus immediately elaborated on what He meant in Matthew 24:44 by telling a parable about a master who ordered his servant to give his household food until the master returned home. By doing his master's will, the servant would prove to be "a faithful and wise servant" (v.45). However, if the servant disobeyed his master and became a violent drunkard, then his master's return would be an unpleasant surprise. Jesus said of the "evil servant" (v.48): "The master of that servant will *come* on a day when he is *not* looking for him and at *an hour* that he is *not* aware of" (v.50). Jesus is saying that the servant who does not obey Him, and becomes an "evil servant" will experience His coming at a time he does not expect. Jesus is implying that this will not be the case for the "faithful and wise servant." This servant will "be ready," and Jesus will not come at a time he does not expect.

We should also notice that Jesus is referring in Matthew

24:44 to His coming that He described in verse 30, and that He said would happen just after the great tribulation (vv.21, 29).

"LIKE TEN VIRGINS" (1)

> *"At that time the kingdom of heaven will be like ten virgins who took their lamps and went out to meet the bridegroom. Five of them were foolish and five were wise. The foolish ones took their lamps but did not take any oil with them. The wise, however, took oil in jars along with their lamps. The bridegroom was a long time in coming, and they all became drowsy and fell asleep. At midnight the cry rang out: 'Here's the bridegroom! Come out to meet him!' Then all the virgins woke up and trimmed their lamps. The foolish ones said to the wise, 'Give us some of your oil; our lamps are going out.' 'No,' they replied, 'there may not be enough for both us and you. Instead, go to those who sell oil and buy some for yourselves.' But while they were on their way to buy the oil, the bridegroom arrived. The virgins who were ready went in with him to the wedding banquet. And the door was shut. Later the others also came. 'Sir! Sir!' they said. 'Open the door for us!' But he replied, 'I tell you the truth, I don't know you.' Therefore keep watch, because you do not know the day or the hour." (Matt. 25:1–13)*

Aren't the virgins in this parable an illustration of two groups of believers in the end time, i.e. those who are ready and are evacuated to heaven several years before Jesus comes to the earth, and those who are not ready who must go through the great tribulation?

This way of thinking ignores the context of the parable in question. Christ's teaching in Matthew 25 has its background in what He told in the previous chapter. He spoke here about His return to the earth in power and glory (Matt. 24:30), which will occur after the great tribulation (Matt. 24:21). Jesus is illustrating this coming in the parable. In these chapters, Jesus does not suggest anything about an evacuation of those who are ready several years before He comes to the earth.

The two groups portrayed are evidently those who enter the kingdom of God that will be set up on the earth when Jesus returns, and those who are excluded from the kingdom. Christ's purpose in telling the parable of the virgins is to warn against foolishness and apostasy in the end time. Those who belong to Him must prepare for His coming.

"LIKE TEN VIRGINS" (2)

Aren't the virgins in the parable in Matthew 25:1–13 types of the saved and the unsaved of Israel when Jesus returns to the earth?

Jesus directed the parable of the virgins to His disciples who became the apostles in the early church. Therefore, it should be viewed as an address to all believers. The parable is meant to shed light on the relation of the believers to Christ's return, and thus keep them ready until He comes.

In verse 6 of the parable, we read, "At midnight the cry rang out: 'Here's the bridegroom! Come out to meet him!'" The word "meet" here is *apántesis* in Greek. The same word is used in 1 Thessalonians 4:17, where we read that the believers will "be caught up . . . in the clouds to meet [*apántesis*] the Lord in the air." Here, we have a clear connection to Paul's words directed to the believers, so we do not have to apply what Jesus said in the parable to the people of Israel.

"LIKE TEN VIRGINS" (3)

According to Jewish wedding customs, the marriage celebration lasts a week. Taking each day of this week to represent a year, doesn't this mean the parable in Matthew 25:1–13 indicates that the coming of Jesus as a Bridegroom will occur seven years prior to His coming after the great tribulation?

When expounding prophetic passages from the Bible we should be wary of employing traditional customs as a source if we want a reliable interpretation. Jesus told His disciples the parable of Him coming as a Bridegroom and being met by the virgins just after having told them He would come and gather His own immediately after a time of great tribulation (Matt. 24:21–31). Therefore, it should be plain to see that Jesus was illustrating what will happen to those who believe in Him when He returns after the great tribulation.

"LIKE TEN VIRGINS" (4)

In biblical times, the bridegroom went with his friends to the childhood home of the bride, where her bridesmaids greeted him. He then escorted his bride and her bridesmaids in a festive procession to his own house. According to the parable of the virgins in Matthew 25:1–13, doesn't this mean that at the return of Christ the church will be fetched to the bridegroom's house, which is heaven?

The whole point of Christ's parable of the virgins is that the believers are to be ready to meet Him when He comes. The most important thing we learn from the parable is not to realize what each detail may mean, but to do what Jesus says in verse 13: "Watch."
Even so, if we are to lay stress upon the events of the

wedding procedure, it looks as if the church will accompany Jesus down to the earth after having met Him in the air (cf. 1 Thess. 4:17), in the same way as the virgins, after having gone out to meet the bridegroom, accompany him back to the childhood home of the bride. Thus, the earth can be likened to the childhood home of the bride where Jesus will come.

Jesus did not mention the bride or a procession to the bridegroom's house in the parable of the virgins. This means we should not make the parable say more than what Jesus intended. We cannot therefore assert that the church will go to heaven when Jesus returns.

We must also be aware that the parable of the virgins in Matthew 25 illustrates what will happen when Jesus returns after the great tribulation (cf. Matt. 24:29–31). In light of this, the "wedding" (Matt. 25:10) represents the celebration of the union of Jesus and His church at the establishment of the kingdom of God on the earth.

"IN THE SYNAGOGUES"

In Christ's end time discourse in Mark 13, we read about synagogues (v.9). Doesn't this mean that He spoke about the Jews, and not the church? Therefore, won't the church be in heaven the last years before Jesus returns to the earth?

The verse referred to says, "You will be beaten in the synagogues." The fact that beatings were carried out in the synagogues tells us that Judaism as a whole rejected the first believers who were all Jews. When Jesus inaugurated the Communion, He said to His disciples, "They will put you out of the synagogues" (John 16:2). This happened because many of the Jewish leaders and their communities did not accept the message of Jesus as Messiah. It was those Jews who believed in Jesus as the Messiah who were beaten in the synagogues and put out of them. This shows that Jesus was talking about believers who make up His church, not the Jewish people as a whole.

In the beginning of the time of the gospel, most of the believers were Jews, but now the Jews are a small minority. The great majority consists of Gentile believers, yet together they comprise the church. This is reflected in Mark 13, where we see that after the reference to believing Jews (v.9) the gospel is preached to "all the nations" (v.10). From this, it should be clear that Mark 13:9 cannot be used to show that the church will be in heaven the last years before Jesus returns to earth.

"THEN THEY WILL SEE THE SON OF MAN"

> *"But in those days, after that tribulation, the sun will be darkened, and the moon will not give its light; the stars will fall, and the powers in the heavens will be shaken.* Then *they will see the Son of Man coming in the clouds with great power and glory. And* then *He will send His angels, and gather together His elect from the four winds, from the farthest part of earth to the farthest part of heaven." (Mark 13:24–27)*

Since the Greek word translated "then" can mean "at that time," doesn't this imply that the gathering of Christ's elect will take place before the aforementioned time of tribulation?

The possibility of understanding the Greek text in this way is ruled out by the context of the verses in question. We read in verse 19, "For in those days there will be *tribulation*, such as has not been since the beginning of the creation which God created until this time, nor ever shall be." In other words, this is the great tribulation. The following verse says, "And unless the Lord shortened those days, no flesh would be saved; but for *the elect's* sake, whom He chose, He shortened those days" (Mark 13:20). This implies that Christ's elect will be present in the great tribulation. They cannot therefore be gathered beforehand. The word "then" in the passage from Mark 13 clearly points to the time *after* the great tribulation. It is at this time the elect will be gathered by the angels when the world sees Jesus "coming in the clouds with great power and glory."

"LEAD US NOT INTO TEMPTATION"

In Luke 11:4, Jesus says we should pray, "And lead us not into temptation." The word "temptation" can be translated "trial." Doesn't this mean that the church will not go into the great tribulation?

The original word translated "temptation" in Luke 11:4 also occurs in Luke 22:28, where Jesus says, "You are those who have stood by me in my *trials*." Paul used the same word in Acts 20:19, where he said he had been "serving the Lord with all humility, with tears and *trials*." It also appears in 1 Peter 4:12: "Dear friends, do not be surprised at the painful *trial* you are suffering, as though something strange were happening to you."

The fact that believers experience trials should suffice to show that Jesus was not thinking of an evacuation before the great tribulation when He taught His disciples to pray in Luke 11.

"RETURN FROM A WEDDING BANQUET"

Since Jesus will return from a wedding (Luke 12:35, 36), this must mean that a wedding takes place before He comes back. Doesn't this imply that the bride, i.e. the church, will be fetched to heaven some time before Jesus returns?

To answer this argument, let us look at the reference in question. Here, Jesus said, "Be dressed ready for service and keep your lamps burning, like men waiting for their master to return from a wedding banquet, so that when he comes and knocks they can immediately open the door for him."

In this passage, Jesus tells His disciples to be "*like* men waiting for their master to return from a wedding banquet." Jesus is comparing the expectancy they should have to His coming with men awaiting their master's return home after being away at a wedding banquet (the context of what Jesus says suggests the master was a guest at the wedding banquet). He also says His disciples are to "be dressed ready for service" keeping their "lamps burning" and "open the door for him" "when he comes and knocks." All these expressions indicate that Jesus was telling a parable. He was not relating literal events.

Those waiting in the parable represent the church because the disciples Jesus was telling the parable to became leaders in the church. Moreover, since the church is the bride of Christ, a literal wedding banquet before the return of Christ without the church participating would not make sense. With this in mind, there is no reason to imply from Christ's parable in Luke 12 that the church will be fetched to heaven some time before He returns.

"THE DAYS OF THE SON OF MAN"

We read in Luke 17:26, "As it was in the days of Noah, so it will be also in the days of the Son of Man." Doesn't the expression "the days of the Son of Man" tell us that Christ's coming will span a period of time, i.e. that several years expire from the time the church is transferred to heaven until Christ comes to the earth?

A parallel passage that can help us understand this verse is Matthew 24:37 & 38:

> But as *the days of Noah* were, so also will the coming of the Son of Man be. For as in *the days before the flood*, they were

eating and drinking, marrying and giving in marriage, until the day that Noah entered the ark, and did not know until *the flood* came and took them all away, so also will *the coming of the Son of Man* be.

We see here that the flood is an illustration of the judgment at "the coming of the Son of Man." It is also apparent that "the days before the flood" are equivalent to "the days of Noah." In Luke 17:26, "the days of Noah" are compared with "the days of the Son of Man." The phrase "the days of the Son of Man" corresponds therefore to "the days before the flood," i.e. the time just prior to the coming of Christ. This period includes the great tribulation that Jesus said precedes His coming (Matt. 24:29, 30).

It is evident that Noah and his family were still on the earth in the days before the flood came. Genesis 7:1–11 informs us they were bringing animals into the ark the last days before the heavens opened and the deluge came. In the same way the flood came and swept away the ungodly, judgment upon the ungodly will come when Jesus is revealed from heaven. Moreover, as Noah and his family were preserved in the ark and saved when the flood came, the church will be preserved and saved by being gathered to Jesus when judgment hits the world at His revelation. Note that in the context of the verses about Noah in Matthew 24, Jesus said very clearly that He will be revealed from heaven "immediately after" the great tribulation (Matt. 24:29, 30).

Because of what we have looked at here, we cannot assume that Christ's coming spans several years, and that the church will be transferred to heaven at the beginning of this time.

"THE DAYS OF NOAH . . . THE DAYS OF LOT"

According to Luke 17:26–30, isn't the flood at the time of Noah and the destruction of Sodom at the time of Lot, types of the great tribulation? Doesn't this mean Noah and Lot are types of the church that will be transferred to heaven before the great tribulation begins?

Here follows the passage from Luke 17:

> And as it was in the days of Noah, so it will be also in the days of the Son of Man: They ate, they drank, they married wives, they were given in marriage, until the day Noah entered the ark, and the flood came and destroyed them all. Likewise as it was also in the days of Lot: They ate, they drank, they bought, they sold, they planted, they built; but on the day that Lot went out of Sodom it rained fire and brimstone from heaven and destroyed them all. Even so will it be in the day when the Son of Man is revealed.

We are informed that "*the day* when the Son of Man is revealed" is compared with "*the day* that Lot went out of Sodom" when the city was burned up. What happens at the revelation of Christ is also compared with the flood at the time of Noah. A reference to Noah and the flood is also found in Matthew 24:37–39. These verses are connected to Christ's revelation that will occur "immediately *after* the tribulation of those days" (v.29) when "all the tribes of the earth will mourn, and they will see the Son of Man coming on the clouds of heaven with power and great glory" (v.30). This is "the day when the Son of Man is revealed" (Luke 17:30).

Against this background, we understand that the flood at the time of Noah, and the fire and brimstone at the time of Lot are types of the judgment at the revelation of Christ immediately *after* the great tribulation. This aligns with what the apostle Peter wrote about the fate of the ungodly world in Noah's time and Sodom in Lot's time as being types of the judgment and perdition of the ungodly (2 Pet. 2:1–6).

When Jesus comes back, He will come with fiery judgment, as the apostle Paul wrote: "The Lord Jesus [will be] revealed from heaven with His mighty angels, in flaming fire taking vengeance on those who do not know God, and on those who do not obey the gospel of our Lord Jesus Christ" (2 Thess. 2:7, 8). At this time, the believers will be caught up in the air to meet Jesus as He returns. In this way, Noah and Lot are types of the church. As they were saved from the judgment of God, the church will be saved when Jesus comes in judgment upon the ungodly: "These shall be punished with everlasting destruction from the presence of the Lord and from the glory of His power, when He comes, in that Day, to be glorified in His saints and to be admired among all those who believe" (2 Thess. 1:9, 10).

The believers will be saved from the fiery judgment that takes place at the revelation of Christ, but this does not mean they will avoid going through the great tribulation before Jesus returns.

"WHEN THESE THINGS BEGIN TO HAPPEN"

In Luke 21, Jesus gives signs that herald His return to the earth "with power and great glory" (v.27). In verse 28, He says, "Now when these things begin to happen, look up and lift up your heads, because your redemption draws near." Doesn't this mean the redemption of the believers will take place when the signs begin to occur, i.e. several years before Jesus comes back to the earth?

This assertion all depends on what Jesus meant when He said, "Now when these things begin to happen." Earlier in the chapter, He mentioned false messiahs (v.8), wars and commotions (vv.9, 10), great earthquakes, famines, pestilences, and great signs from heaven (v.11). In verse 12, He said, "But before all this, they will lay hands on you and persecute you." From here to verse 19, Jesus elaborated on the persecution of the believers. He then describes the desolation of Jerusalem (vv.20–23) and its being trampled on by the Gentiles (v.24). Then He mentions signs in the sun, in the moon, and in the stars (v.25), the powers of the heavens being shaken (v.26) and Him coming in a cloud with power and great glory (v.27). It is then Jesus says, "Now when *these things* begin to happen, look up and lift your heads, because your redemption draws near" (v.28).

Further on in verse 31, Jesus says, "When you *see these things* happening." This is apparently a reference to the things He had just told about. Since the believers must be present to *see* these things happen, their redemption cannot take place at the beginning of what Jesus talked about. It should then be clear that when Jesus said, "Now when these things begin to happen," He had in mind what He had just said:

> And there will be *signs in the sun, in the moon, and in the stars*; and on the earth distress of nations, with perplexity, *the sea and the waves roaring*; men's hearts failing them from fear and the expectation of those things which are coming on the earth, for *the powers of the heaven will be shaken.* Then they will see the Son of Man coming in a cloud with power and great glory. (Luke 21:25–27)

Jesus also says the cosmic signs He describes here will happen just after the great tribulation:

> But *in those days, after that tribulation, the sun will be darkened, and the moon will not give its light; the stars of heaven will fall, and the powers in heaven will be shaken.* Then they will see the Son of Man coming in the clouds with great power and glory. And then He will send His angels, and gather together His elect. (Mark 13:24–27)

It is plain to see that the redemption of the believers occurs when Jesus is revealed and His glory is visible in the clouds after the great tribulation. This is also brought out by what John writes: "We know that when He is revealed, we shall be like Him, for we shall see Him as He is" (1 John 3:2). Therefore, the time for looking up and lifting up one's head is when the sun and the moon are darkened, the stars fall, the sea and the waves roar, and the powers of heaven are shaken. When these things begin to happen, then the coming of Jesus and the redemption of the believers is drawing near.

From the Letters

"IN THE TWINKLING OF AN EYE"

Doesn't 1 Corinthians 15:51 & 52 inform us the rapture is a mysterious event that was revealed to Paul, unlike the glorious appearing of Christ after the great tribulation?

Let us look at the verses mentioned:

> Listen, I tell you a mystery: We will not all sleep, but we will all be changed—in a flash, in the twinkling of an eye, at the last trumpet. For the trumpet will sound, the dead will be raised imperishable, and we will be changed.

It is readily seen that the mystery addressed here is the transformation of the bodies of the believers still alive at the sounding of the trumpet when Jesus comes. The mystery does not concern the actual catching up because this is not mentioned in the passage. We are told it is the act of being changed that will happen in the twinkling of an eye, not the gathering of the believers to meet Jesus. Paul is therefore not introducing a mysterious coming of Christ prior to His coming after the great tribulation. He is simply telling what will immediately precede the gathering of the believers when Jesus returns. The transformation of the believers' bodies will make it possible for them to be gathered to Jesus in the clouds when He comes.

Paul continues in 1 Corinthians 15 by saying that a prophecy in Isaiah 25:8 will be fulfilled when the transformation of the believers' bodies occurs:

> When this corruptible has put on incorruption, and this mortal has put on immortality, then shall be brought to pass the saying that is written: '*Death is swallowed up in victory.*' (1 Cor. 15:54)

Let us look at the setting of this prophecy in the book of Isaiah. Chapter 24 describes massive upheavals on the earth that will happen in the end time: "Therefore the curse has devoured the earth, and those who dwell in it are desolate. Therefore the inhabitants of the earth are burned, and few men are left. . . . The earth is violently broken, the earth is split open, the earth is shaken exceedingly" (Is. 24:6, 19). These verses describe some of the final events of the great tribulation. The last verse in the chapter says, "Then the moon will be disgraced and the sun ashamed; for the Lord of hosts will reign on Mount Zion and in Jerusalem and before His elders, gloriously" (Is. 24:23). This is the coming of Christ to reign on the earth after the signs in the sun and the moon (cf. Matt. 24:29). Just a few verses later, we read the prophecy, "He will swallow up death in victory" (Is. 25:8). The context tells us that this prophecy will be fulfilled at the coming of Christ after the great tribulation. Paul connects the fulfillment of this prophecy to the rapture, thus indicating that the rapture will occur after the great tribulation.

When Paul wrote about the rapture in 1 Thessalonians 4:17, he introduced it by saying, "The Lord himself will come down from heaven, with a loud command, with the voice of the archangel and with the trumpet call of God" (v.16). This can be compared to the procedure used when a king went to visit a city. The king's herald would go before him to the city walls to announce with a shout and trumpet blast the coming of the king. This underlines that the coming of Christ is a loud public event, not something that will take place in a mysterious fashion. The scene Paul describes fits Christ's teaching of Him coming after the great tribulation "with power and great glory" (Matt. 24:30) and "with a great sound of a trumpet" (Matt. 24:31). This is when the believers "shall all be changed—in a moment, in the twinkling of an eye, at the last trumpet" (1 Cor. 15:51).

"HE MADE KNOWN TO ME THE MYSTERY"

Doesn't Ephesians 3:3–5 say the church is a mystery that was revealed to the apostle Paul? Doesn't this mean that what Jesus taught His disciples concerning the end time is not about the church?

In the passage in question, Paul writes:

> By revelation He made known to me the mystery (as I have briefly written already, by which, when you read, you may understand my knowledge in the mystery of Christ), which in other ages was not made known to the sons of men, as it has now been revealed by the Spirit to His holy apostles and prophets. (Eph. 3:3–5)

Paul calls the mystery made known to him, "the mystery of Christ," which he wrote about in the first two chapters of his letter to the Ephesians. He says the mystery of Christ was not only revealed to him, but also to Christ's other apostles and prophets.

Then Paul tells us what the mystery of Christ entails: ". . . that the Gentiles should be fellow heirs, of the same body, and partakers of His promise in Christ through the gospel" (Eph. 3:6). Paul is saying the mystery he was given knowledge of is the inclusion of the Gentiles in the body of Christ, which is the church of Christ. Clearly, the mystery is not the church itself, which originally comprised of only Jewish believers.

In his letter to the Colossians, Paul writes again about the mystery:

> I became a minister according to the stewardship from God which was given to me for you, to fulfill the word of God, the mystery which has been hidden from ages and from generations, but now has been revealed to His saints. To them God willed to make known what are the riches of the glory of

this mystery among the Gentiles: which is Christ in you, the hope of glory. (Col. 1:25–27)

Paul says here the mystery concerns the believing Gentiles—their sharing in the hope of receiving eternal glory along with believing Jews. Again, it is evident that the mystery, once hidden and now revealed, is not the church itself, but is Christ in Gentile believers.

Concerning the church itself, Jesus was the One who revealed the concept of it. He said, "I will build My church" (Matt. 16:18). Jesus started laying its foundations by calling men to follow Him who later became apostles. At that time, Christ's Jewish disciples did not realize that Gentiles would become one with them in believing in Him. However, Jesus hinted at this in parabolic form:

And other sheep I have [*Gentiles who would become believers*] which are not of this fold [*those who believed in Jesus among the Jews*]; them also I must bring, and they will hear My voice; and there will be one flock [*the church*] and one shepherd [*Jesus*]. (John 10:16)

Then we have Christ's commission to His disciples after His resurrection: "Go into all the world and preach the gospel to every creature. He who believes and is baptized will be saved" (Mark 16:15–16). Here, Jesus alludes to Gentiles receiving the gospel, being baptized, and thus being joined to the church of baptized Jewish believers.

From what we have looked at, it is apparent that the mystery Paul received extended revelation about was the inclusion of Gentiles in the church through faith in Christ. The church itself was evidently not a mystery revealed to the apostle Paul because Jesus said He was going to construct it. He started with His Jewish disciples who became leaders and teachers in His church. Thus, it is plain to see that what Jesus taught His disciples concerning the end time is relevant to the church.

"THE DAY OF CHRIST"

We read in the Bible about "the day of Christ" (e.g. Phil. 1:10), as well as "the day of the Lord" (e.g. 1 Thess. 5:2). Don't these two expressions signify two different aspects of the return of Christ, i.e. "the day of Christ" concerns the transfer of the believers to heaven before the great tribulation, and "the day of the Lord" points to the return of Christ to the earth after the great tribulation?

According to the Bible's own testimony, these two expressions are identical in meaning. There is no reason to separate them, since they are two of several expressions that cover the same subject. These are "*the day* of Jesus *Christ*" (Phil. 1:6), "*the day of* our *Lord* Jesus *Christ*" (1 Cor. 1:8), and "*the day of the Lord* Jesus" (1 Cor. 5:5; 2 Cor. 1:14). It is also quite simply called "*the Day*" (1 Cor. 3:13; Heb. 10:25) or "that *Day*" (2 Thess. 1:10; 2 Tim. 1:12, 18; 4:8). Thus, the term "the day of Christ" is just another way of saying "the day of the Lord." This conclusion is supported by the fact that in some Bibles the term "the day of Christ" in 2 Thessalonians 2:2 is rendered "the day of the Lord." These two terms should therefore not be separated neither in time nor in content.

Concerning the term "the day of the Lord," we see from what Paul writes that Jesus will come and gather all the believers to Himself on "the day of the Lord" (1 Thess. 4:13–17; 5:2). We also see that Jesus will destroy the Antichrist on "the day of the Lord" (2 Thess. 2:2, 8). We understand from this that both these incidents will happen when Jesus returns after the great tribulation.

"LOOK FOR THE SAVIOR"

Doesn't the fact that we "look for the Savior" (Phil. 3:20 KJV) tell us to anticipate the coming of Christ at any moment?

The Greek word translated "look for" is *apekdechomai*. This word is a compound of *apo* (away from) and *ekdechomai* (to await). It means to await something at a distance with anticipation. Most Bible translations render it "wait for" rather than "look for." In the other occurrences of this Greek word in the KJV, it is usually rendered "wait."

In Romans 8:19, the Greek word *apekdechomai* is used about the creation awaiting the manifestation of the sons of God. The restoration of the creation occurs when Jesus returns after the great tribulation. All agree that certain prophesied events must take place before the restoration of the creation. It cannot occur at any moment.

The Greek term is also used in 1 Peter 3:20 of God waiting for Noah to finish the ark. Obviously, God did not expect him to be done at any moment. This illustrates that the use of the word *apekdechomai* does not mean that what is expected may happen at any moment.

In the light of the above, Paul's exhortation does not imply that Jesus can come at any moment. Rather, it means that we are to, as the New King James Version puts it, "eagerly wait for the Savior."

"WITH ALL HIS SAINTS"

In 1 Thessalonians 3:13, we read of "the coming of our Lord Jesus Christ with all His saints." What else could this refer to than the believers who are fetched to heaven before the great tribulation, and who descend with Christ from heaven after the great tribulation?

The whole verse reads, "So that He may establish your hearts blameless in holiness before our God and Father at the coming of our Lord Jesus Christ with all His saints." Here, we see that believers in the church who will be established blameless in holiness at Christ's coming are distinguished from "all His saints" who come with Him. In the next chapter, it says concerning the return of Christ, "God will *bring with Him* those who sleep in Jesus" (4:14). Apparently, they are the saints spoken of in 1 Thessalonians 3:13 who will be with Jesus when He comes. All the spirits of those who died believing in Jesus will come with Him to receive their resurrection bodies (cf. 1 Thess. 4:16; 1 Cor. 15:51–53). Together with the believers still alive who are changed, they will be caught up in the clouds to accompany Jesus at His arrival to the earth (cf. 1 Thess. 4:17), which happens after the great tribulation. Thus, 1 Thessalonians 3:13 cannot be used to prove that the believers will be fetched to heaven before the great tribulation.

"COMFORT ONE ANOTHER"

Paul writes that the believers are to comfort one another in view of the return of Christ (1 Thess. 4:18). If Christ isn't going to come before the great tribulation, how can the message of the return of Christ be one of comfort?

The reason Paul mentioned comfort in connection with the return of Christ has not initially anything to do with tribulation in the end time. By reading from verse 13 in 1 Thessalonians 4, we see that Paul wanted to inform the believers in Thessalonica about what will happen to those in the church who had died as believers in Jesus (they are mentioned in verses 13, 14, 15, 16, and 17). Paul found it necessary to write about this because the church apparently thought those who had died among them would miss out on the return of Christ.

Paul showed that believers who "are asleep," i.e. have died, will be resurrected (v.16) just ahead of the gathering of the believers at Christ's return (v.17). In this way, Paul gave the church the comfort they needed because of their deceased. They did not need to "sorrow as others who have no hope" (v.13). This is why the chapter ends with these words: "Therefore comfort one another with these words" (v.18). Thus, this statement concerning the resurrection of believers who have died does not show that Jesus will come before the great tribulation.

"THE DAY OF THE LORD"

Doesn't the expression "the day of the Lord" in 1 Thessalonians 5:2 mean the great tribulation? And since the rapture described in 1 Thessalonians 4:17 occurs at the beginning of the day of the Lord, doesn't this mean that the rapture occurs before the great tribulation?

A close examination of Scripture shows that this theory is found wanting. In Joel 2:30 & 31, we read:

> And I will show wonders in the heavens and in the earth: Blood and fire and pillars of smoke. The sun shall be turned into darkness, and the moon into blood, *before* the coming of the great and terrible *day of the Lord*.

It is quite clear from these verses that the signs in the sun and the moon will occur *before* the day of the Lord. According to Jesus, these signs will occur immediately *after* the great tribulation:

> Immediately *after the tribulation* of those days the sun will be darkened, and the moon will not give its light. . . . and then all the tribes of the earth will mourn, and they will see the Son of Man coming on the clouds of heaven with power and great glory. (Matt. 24:29, 30)

From this, we understand that the day of the Lord is synonymous with the Lord's return after the great tribulation. This means the day of the Lord cannot be the same as the great tribulation, as the following outline of the aforementioned verses shows:

	1.	2.	3.
JOEL:	Blood and fire	The sun and the moon are darkened	The day of the Lord
JESUS:	Great tribulation	The sun and the moon are darkened	The coming of the Lord

The apostle Paul tells us "the man of sin" (the Antichrist) will be revealed *before* the coming of the "day of the Lord" (2 Thess. 2:2, 3). When the day of the Lord comes, Jesus will destroy the Antichrist "with the breath of His mouth" (v.8). This will occur after the great tribulation, which again means the day of the Lord cannot be identified with the great tribulation itself.

According to Malachi 4:5, another character will appear before the day of the Lord: "Behold, I will send you Elijah the prophet *before* the coming of the great and dreadful day of the Lord" (Mal. 4:5). It is very likely that this prophet refers to one of the two prophets of God who will minister in the great tribulation (Rev. 11:10). These prophets will perform signs that are similar to the signs the prophet Elijah performed (Rev. 11:5 / 2 Kings 1:10; Rev. 11:6 / 1 Kings 17:1). That a prophet of God will appear in the great tribulation *before* the day of the Lord comes points to the fact that the day of the Lord comes *after* the great tribulation.

Paul wrote concerning the day of the Lord, "For you yourselves know perfectly that the day of the Lord so comes as a thief in the night" (1 Thess. 5:2). The believers Paul wrote to knew that the day of the Lord would come unexpectedly "as a thief in the night" because he had told them beforehand. However, he does point out it is the ungodly that are going to experience the day of the Lord as a thief (v.4), i.e. unexpectedly. Paul is probably referring to Christ's words about His coming as a thief in Matthew 24:43. According to verse 30, this concerns Christ's descent in glory to the earth after the great tribulation. Again, we see the day of the Lord is not the great tribulation, but comes after this time at Christ's glorious revelation.

Since the rapture of the believers to meet Jesus in the air occurs at the commencement of the day of the Lord, and the day of the Lord comes after the great tribulation, this means the rapture will occur after the great tribulation at Christ's coming.

"PEACE AND SAFETY"

In 1 Thessalonians 5:2, we read about "the day of the Lord." Then in verse 3, we read about "peace and safety" and "sudden destruction." Isn't this an indication that the day of the Lord will begin with a time of peace that will change into a time of tribulation? We also read that the day of the Lord begins with the rapture (1 Thess. 4:17). Doesn't this mean the rapture will occur before both the time of peace and the time of tribulation?

The idea that the day of the Lord consists of a time of peace followed by a time of tribulation is based on a defective understanding of the whole passage where the words, "Peace and safety" occur. The following is the passage that we need to take a closer look at:

> For you yourselves know perfectly that the day of the Lord so comes as a thief in the night. For when they say, 'Peace and safety!' then sudden destruction comes upon them, as labor pains upon a pregnant woman. And they shall not escape. But you, brethren, are not in darkness, so that this Day should overtake you as a thief. (1 Thess. 5:2–4)

It is evident that the day of the Lord will come unexpectedly and suddenly on those who are "in darkness." It will bring "sudden destruction" that "comes upon them, as labor pains upon a pregnant woman." This "sudden destruction" will befall those who had just said, "Peace and safety!" Therefore, to insist that the day of the Lord begins with a time of peace is contrary to the context. Clearly, the day of the Lord begins with "sudden destruction."

Concerning the statement, "For when they say, 'Peace and safety,'" it is necessary to point out that it does not have to reflect the actual condition of the world before the day of the Lord comes. In Jeremiah 6:13 & 14, we read, "From the prophet even to the priest, everyone deals falsely. They have also healed the hurt of My people slightly, *saying, 'Peace*, peace!' when there is no peace." In other words, there was not going to be any peace although the false prophets and the priests said there would be. This seems to reflect how it will be in the last days. People will speak of peace and security, but it will not turn out that way.

As for the phrase, "sudden destruction [Gk. *olethros*]," 2 Thessalonians 1:7–9 shows us that it should not be understood as a time of tribulation:

> [God will] give you who are troubled rest with us when the Lord Jesus is revealed from heaven with His mighty angels, in flaming fire taking vengeance on those who do not know God, and on those who do not obey the gospel of our Lord Jesus Christ. These shall be punished with everlasting destruction [Gk. *olethron*] from the presence of the Lord and from the glory of His power.

From the Greek text, we understand that "sudden destruction" in 1 Thessalonians 5:3 is equivalent to "everlasting destruction" in 2 Thessalonians 1:9. According to the text, this will occur when the day of the Lord comes. The passage in 2 Thessalonians 1 is a description of the revelation of Christ after the great tribulation. This means the day of the Lord will come after the great tribulation, and is therefore not equivalent to the actual time of tribulation itself. (See the answer to the previous argument for more on when the day of the Lord begins.)

Paul wrote in 1 Thessalonians 5:4 that "this Day" (the day of the Lord) should not overtake the believers "as a thief," i.e.

unexpectedly and suddenly. It is in this connection Paul says, "Sudden destruction comes upon" (i.e. overtakes) the unbelievers (v.3). This shows that the day of the Lord will mean destruction for unbelievers. On the other hand, for believers it will mean being caught up in the air to meet Jesus when He comes. And according to what we have deduced, this will happen after the great tribulation.

"GOD DID NOT APPOINT US TO WRATH"

In 1 Thessalonians 5:9, we read, "For God did not appoint us to wrath." Doesn't this mean that the church will not be present in the great tribulation?

When Paul writes, "For God did not appoint us to wrath," the word "For" connects what he says here to the end of the previous verse, where he mentions "the hope of salvation" (v.8). Paul is saying that believers are destined for salvation, and not the wrath of God. He underlines this in verse 9: "For God did not appoint us to wrath, *but to obtain salvation*." Since Paul contrasts wrath with salvation, it is apparent that he uses the word "wrath" in reference to damnation, as he does in Romans 2:5, where he speaks of all the unsaved throughout history storing up "wrath" for judgment day. In Romans 5:9, he says of all believers throughout history, "We shall be *saved from wrath* through Him." Therefore, Paul does not use the word "wrath" to denote a short period of tribulation in the end time; it is the opposite of eternal life, as John 3:36 shows: "He who does not believe the Son shall not see life, but the *wrath* of God abides on him." Thus, Paul is not saying in 1 Thessalonians 5:9 that believers are not appointed to tribulation—whether minor or great. This is clear from what he states earlier in the same letter: "No one should be shaken by these afflictions; for you yourselves know that we are *appointed to* this. For, in fact, we told you before when we were with you that we would suffer *tribulation*" (1 Thess. 3:3, 4).

"SHAKEN IN MIND OR TROUBLED"

"Now, brethren, concerning the coming of our Lord Jesus Christ and our gathering together to Him, we ask you, not to be soon shaken in mind or troubled, either by spirit or by word or by letter, as if from us, as though the day of Christ had come." (2 Thess. 2:1, 2)

The believers had received a false report, which said that "the day of Christ had come." Since this troubled them, doesn't this mean they believed Christ had come and fetched His true church, and they now had to go through the tribulation period?

The report the church in Thessalonica had received caused Paul to write that they should not be troubled. However, this does not have to mean they were troubled by the thought of experiencing tribulation. Paul had written to them, "We told you before when we were with you that we would suffer tribulation" (1 Thess. 3:4). In his second letter to them, he wrote, "We ourselves boast of you among the churches of God for your patience and faith in all your persecutions and tribulations that you endure" (2 Thess. 1:4). It does not therefore appear to be the thought of tribulation that troubled the church.

The false report had allegedly come from Paul, Silas and Timothy ("as if from us" – 2 Thess. 2:2; cf. 2 Thess. 1:1). It is unthinkable they of all people would have been excluded if the issue was that Jesus had come and fetched His true church to heaven. Therefore, I think it highly unlikely that the report said Jesus had already come and gone.

The church in Thessalonica had heard in the false report that "the day of Christ had come." The expression "had come" (Gk. *enésteken*) was partially used in older writings of what we could call the present year. We can therefore assume it was asserted Jesus would come almost immediately, not that He had already come. This is reflected in the KJV and ASV, where the Greek expression is translated "is at hand," i.e. 'has become imminent.'

Apparently, an exaggerated expectation of the return of Christ had spread in the church resulting in undue excitement. Some of them had even stopped working since they believed that Jesus would come at once (2 Thess. 3:10, 11). The report unsettled and alarmed many of them because they were presumably unprepared and unsure concerning what was about to happen. They were "shaken in mind" (2 Thess. 2:2) because of their faulty understanding of the situation. Paul wrote his second letter to them to bring the whole matter into balance. He corrects the church and shows them that the day of Christ will not come unannounced. There are certain signs the believers will see: "Let no one deceive you by any means; for that Day will not come unless the falling away comes *first*, and the man of sin is revealed, the son of perdition" (2 Thess. 2:3). Here, Paul reminded the Thessalonians that the day of Christ ("that Day") had not yet come because there were two things that had to take place beforehand, namely the falling away and the appearance of "the man of sin" (the Antichrist).

According to 1 Thessalonians 4:16–5:2, the day of Christ will feature the coming of Christ and the gathering of the believers to meet Him. Since the falling away and the appearance of the Antichrist will occur prior to the day of Christ, this means these two things will happen before Christ's coming and the gathering of the believers. The order of events will therefore be:

1. The falling away
2. The appearance of the Antichrist
3. The day of Christ when Christ returns

When Christ comes back the believers "who are troubled" will be given "rest" (2 Thess. 1:7). They will be "caught up . . . in the clouds to meet the Lord in the air" (1 Thess. 4:17). In this way they will not be affected by the vengeance of God that befalls the ungodly "when the Lord Jesus is revealed from heaven with His mighty angels, in flaming fire taking vengeance on those who do not know God" (2 Thess. 1:7, 8). This is when Jesus consumes the Antichrist "with the breath of His mouth"

(2 Thess. 2:8).

Paul's concern in 2 Thessalonians 2 is to show that the return of Christ and the gathering together of the believers would not take place immediately because the Antichrist will appear first. He had in fact already explained this to the believers in Thessalonica: "Do you not remember that when I was with you I told you these things?" (v.5). Because of this, they could ignore the false report that had come to them.

"THE MAN OF SIN"

Won't the appearance of the Antichrist be the first main event on "the day of Christ," according to 2 Thessalonians 2:1–3?

The verses referred to are the following:

> Now, brethren, concerning the coming of our Lord Jesus Christ and our gathering together to Him, we ask you, not to be soon shaken in mind or troubled, either by spirit or by word or by letter as if from us as though the day of Christ had come. Let no one deceive you by any means; for that Day will not come unless the falling away comes first, and the man of sin is revealed, the son of perdition.

Paul says very clearly here that the day of Christ had not yet come because the appearance of "the man of sin" (the Antichrist) had not yet happened. In other words, the appearance of the Antichrist occurs *before* the day of Christ comes. It is not to be understood as the first thing to happen when "that Day" comes.

According to 1 Thessalonians 4:16–5:2, the first events on the day of Christ are the coming of Christ, the resurrection of the dead in Christ, and the catching up of the believers to meet Him in the clouds. After Paul had written about these events at the end of chapter 4, he connects them in chapter 5 to "the day of the

Lord [i.e. Christ]" (v.2). What then happens is found in 2 Thessalonians 2:8, where we read of "the lawless one [the Antichrist] . . . whom the Lord Jesus will overthrow with the breath of his mouth and destroy by the splendor of his coming." Thus, the day of Christ brings the destruction of the Antichrist, not his appearance.

"THE COMING OF OUR LORD"

In 2 Thessalonians 2:1, we read of "the coming [Gk. tes parousias] of our Lord Jesus Christ and our gathering together to Him." In verse 8, we read of Christ destroying the Antichrist with "the brightness of His coming [Gk. epiphaneia tes parousias]." Don't these two Greek terms show that Christ's coming will occur in two acts, the first being a secret coming to fetch the church to heaven before the great tribulation, the second being a public appearance for the world after the great tribulation?

If we take a closer look at the Greek terms mentioned, we see there is no real backing for such a conclusion.

The term *parousia* conveys the meaning of 'presence' (2 Cor. 10:10; Phil. 2:12), and it is used of any person's arrival (1 Cor. 16:17; 2 Cor. 7:6, 7). In classic Greek, this word was used of a deity's arrival at a cult-site, or a king's arrival in a city. There isn't anything in the word to support the idea of a secret coming. In fact, the term *parousia* is used in Matthew 24:3 & 27 of Christ's glorious return, which Christ Himself says will take place *after* the great tribulation (Matt. 24:21, 29, 30). It is also used by Paul in 1 Thessalonians 4:15 before describing the catching up of the believers to Jesus in the clouds in verse 17.

The term *epiphaneia* carries the meaning of 'to show forth' or 'appearance.' Besides being used together with *parousia*, it is also used independently of the return of Christ, e.g. in 2 Timothy 4:8, where Paul writes of "all who have loved His appearing [*epiphaneia*]," and in Titus 2:13, where he writes of the "glorious appearing [*epiphaneia*] of our great God and Savior Jesus Christ." It is therefore apparent that the believers are awaiting Christ's *epiphaneia*. This Greek term is therefore practically synonymous with *parousia*.

From the above we understand that *tes parousias* in 2 Thessalonians 2:1, when the believers will be gathered to Jesus, is not a coming that will occur several years before *epiphaneia tes parousias* in verse 8. The purpose of the expanded term in verse 8 is to emphasize "the brightness" of Christ's coming in relation to the destruction of the Antichrist. Therefore, Paul is not referring to a secret coming before the great tribulation in verse 1; he is speaking here of the same return of Christ as in verse 8. That Paul wrote about the same coming of Christ in verses 1 and 8 of 2 Thessalonians 2, is illustrated by his writing of the same coming of Christ in verses 1 and 8 of 2 Timothy 4, where the term "His appearing [*epiphaneia*]" occurs in both verses.

When describing Christ's return, a third Greek term is also used—*apokalupsis*, which means 'revelation.' One of the places Paul uses this word is 2 Thessalonians 1:7, where he writes that God will give the troubled believers rest "when the Lord Jesus is revealed [*apokalupsei*] from heaven with His mighty angels."

By closely studying the Bible, we see that these three Greek words are used interchangeably when speaking of the return of Christ. For example, we read, "Establish your hearts, for the coming [*parousia*] of the Lord is at hand" (James 5:8); "Keep this command without spot, blameless until our Lord Jesus Christ's appearing [*epiphaneia*]" (1 Tim. 6:14); ". . . eagerly waiting for the revelation [*apokalupsis*] of our Lord Jesus Christ" (1 Cor. 1:7). That these words are used interchangeably is also illustrated by the use of both *apokalupsis* and *parousia* concerning the Antichrist. In 2 Thessalonians 2:3 & 6 we read that "the man of sin" will be "revealed" (*apokalyfthe*), and verse 9 tells of his "coming" (*parousia*). Both these words have the same meaning, as they have when used of the return of Christ.

I conclude that 2 Thessalonians 2 does not speak of the return of Christ being divided into two acts, with one coming before the great tribulation, and one after that time. Only one coming of Christ is portrayed when the believers will be gathered to Him, and the Antichrist destroyed—after the great tribulation.

"THE BLESSED HOPE"

In Titus 2:13, we read that the believers should be "looking for the blessed hope and glorious appearing of our great God and Savior Jesus Christ." Isn't "the blessed hope" deliverance from the great tribulation by being fetched to heaven beforehand?

The term "hope" is connected to the return of Christ, but it does not imply escaping tribulations and difficult times before Jesus returns. Jesus Himself said, "In the world you will have tribulation" (John 16:33). Moreover, Paul stated, "We must through many tribulations enter the kingdom of God" (Acts 14:22).

As for the hope of the believers, we read, "But we know that when he appears, we shall be like him, for we shall see him as he is. Everyone who has *this hope* in him purifies himself, just as he is pure" (1 John 3:2, 3). Thus, the hope of the believer is to become like Jesus at His appearing. In this regard, Paul encourages his readers to "eagerly wait for the Savior, the Lord Jesus Christ, who will transform our lowly body that it may be conformed to His glorious body" (Phil. 3:20, 21). The expression "the blessed hope" concerns therefore the transformation of the believers' bodies at Christ's "glorious appearing" (Titus 2:13).

Paul wrote that believers experiencing "persecutions and tribulations" (2 Thess. 1:4) would be given "rest . . . when the Lord Jesus is revealed from heaven with His mighty angels" (2 Thess. 1:7). Evidently, this constitutes "the blessed hope," not deliverance from the great tribulation by being fetched to heaven beforehand.

We should also notice also that "the blessed hope" in Titus 2:13 is connected to the phrase "*hope* of eternal life" in Titus 1:2 and "the *hope* of eternal life" in Titus 3:7. Clearly, Paul had the hope of eternal life in mind when he wrote "the blessed hope." This will be a reality when Jesus comes in glory after the great tribulation, and the believers are transformed to be like Him forever.

"TRANSLATED"

We read in Hebrews 11:5, "By faith Enoch was translated so that he did not see death, and was not found because God had translated him." Isn't Enoch a type of the church that will be translated to heaven at the return of Christ?

Although Enoch was translated, we have to be aware that a type cannot decide what is going to take place, in the same way as a shadow cannot decide what casts the shadow. Furthermore, only verses of Scripture that actually speak of the return of Jesus can be used to accurately teach about His return, and not verses that supposedly illustrate what will happen when He returns. If we use Scripture in this tentative way, we can make it say whatever we want it to say.

The Bible says that at the return of Christ the believers will be "caught up . . . in the clouds . . . in the air" (1 Thess. 4:17). There, the believers are going to "meet the Lord" who will "descend from heaven" (v.16). These verses do not say the believers are going to be transported to heaven or to outer space, but only that they meet Jesus in the air.

A type that is apparently closer to what will happen to the church at the return of Christ, is what happened to Philip the evangelist. After having baptized the eunuch, we read, "Now when they came up out of the water, the Spirit of the Lord *caught* Philip *away*, so that the eunuch saw him no more; and he went on his way rejoicing. But Philip was found at Azotus" (Acts 8:39, 40). Philip was caught up in the air and then brought down at another place. This seems to mirror what is going to happen at the return of Christ. The believers from the whole world will be "caught up . . . in the clouds to meet the Lord in the air" (1 Tess. 4:17). They will then accompany Jesus in His descent to Jerusalem when "His feet will stand on the Mount of Olives" (Zech. 14:4).

From the Book of Revelation

"HE IS COMING WITH CLOUDS"

In Revelation 1:7, we read, "Behold, He is coming with clouds, and every eye will see Him." Don't the clouds mentioned here depict the white robes of the believers who come with Christ from heaven, where they were transferred to before the great tribulation?

The word "cloud" is sometimes used metaphorically in the Bible. For example, in Hebrews 12:1, we read of a "cloud of witnesses," which is a plain reference to people. However, when it comes to Revelation 1:7, there is no reason to understand the word "clouds" metaphorically. This is because several other references in the Bible concerning the return of Christ mention literal clouds. In Mark 13:26, we read that Jesus will be seen "coming in the *clouds*," and Luke 21:27 says that Jesus will come "in a *cloud* with power and great glory." We also read that at the return of Christ the believers will be "caught up . . . in the *clouds* to meet the Lord in the air" (1 Thess. 4:17). None of these Scripture references gives the impression of anything other than literal clouds.

At His ascension, Jesus was taken up while His disciples watched, "and a *cloud* received Him out of their sight" (Acts 1:9). Two angels appeared to the disciples and told them that Jesus would "come in like manner" as they saw Him go into heaven (v.11). This tells us Jesus will appear in a cloud when He comes, thus indicating that Revelation 1:7 does not refer to white robes. We can therefore dismiss this verse as evidence of a transfer of believers to heaven before the great tribulation.

"THINGS WHICH WILL TAKE PLACE AFTER THIS"

In Revelation 1:19, Christ says to John, "Write the things which you have seen, and the things which are, and the things which will take place after this." The "things which you have seen" point to John's vision of the glorified Christ in chapter 1, while "the things which are" concern the churches described in chapters 2 and 3. From the fourth chapter "the things which take place after this" are described. Don't these things point to what will happen after the church age? The word 'church' is not mentioned again until chapter 22, which is the last chapter in the book. Doesn't this mean the church is in heaven during the great tribulation (described in Revelation 6–18)?

The following shows that even though the word "church" does not occur in Revelation 4–21, this does not necessarily mean that the church is not on the earth in the great tribulation. (By 'church,' we mean the universal church as expressed by Paul in Ephesians 1:22 & 23, where he says that God gave Jesus "to be the head of all things to the *church*, which is His body.")

A study of the book of Revelation reveals that only local churches are referred to wherever the word "church" occurs. For example, we read about "the church of Ephesus" (2:1), one of "the seven churches" (1:4, 11, 20), otherwise called "the churches" (2:7; 22:16). Although churches are mentioned, the emphasis in John's writing is placed on each believer in the churches. We see this by the giving of promises to "him who overcomes" (2:7, 11, 17, 26; 3:5, 12, 21). Later in the book, John mentions people called "brethren" (6:11; 12:10; 19:10), "those who keep the commandments of God and the faith of Jesus" (14:12), "the martyrs of Jesus" (17:6), and "the saints" (13:7, 10;

14:12; 17:6). These designations point to believers, and it is precisely believers who make up the church, both locally and universally. Thus, we have here an indication of the church being present on the earth in the main part of the book of Revelation.

When Jesus says, "write . . . the things which will take place after this," He can simply be referring to what was to be shown John after the messages to the churches. This does not mean, however, that what John saw from the fourth chapter onwards does not concern the churches. The following helps us to see why:

In chapter 3, Jesus says to the angel of the church in Sardis: "If you will not *watch, I will come upon you as a thief,* and you will not know what hour I will come upon you. You have a few names even in Sardis who have not defiled their *garments*; and they shall *walk* with Me in white, for they are worthy" (vv.3, 4). This can be compared with what Jesus says in chapter 16: "Behold, *I am coming as a thief.* Blessed is he who *watches*, and keeps his *garments*, lest he *walk* naked and they see his shame" (v.15). Christ's statement here is made in connection with events in the great tribulation, as the next verse shows: "And they gathered them together to the place called in Hebrew, Armageddon" (v.16). Notice there are several things common to both of Christ's utterances; i.e. He will come "as a thief," and the words "watch," "garments," and "walk." It is plain to see that Jesus is speaking of the same things in both instances; the same use of words in both chapter 3 and chapter 16 mean that the church is addressed in both cases. This tells us the present 'church age' does not end before the great tribulation, but continues right up to the coming of Christ back to the earth as described in chapter 19.

"INTO GREAT TRIBULATION"

In Revelation 2:20, we read about the "woman Jezebel, who calls herself a prophetess." Jesus says He will cast "those who commit adultery with her into great tribulation" (Rev. 2:22).

Isn't Jesus saying that only believers who are spiritually adulterous will enter into the great tribulation?

The verses referred to are part of a message from Jesus that John was to convey to the church in Thyatira. Here is the relevant passage:

> "Nevertheless I have a few things against you, because you allow that woman Jezebel, who calls herself a prophetess, to teach and seduce My servants to commit sexual immorality and eat things sacrificed to idols. And I gave her time to repent of her sexual immorality, and she did not repent. Indeed I will cast her into a sickbed, and those who commit adultery with her into great tribulation, unless they repent of their deeds." (Rev. 2:20–22)

It is clear that Jesus was addressing a situation in the church in Thyatira in the Roman province of Asia in western Turkey (cf. Rev. 1:11) at the time of the apostle John. A false prophetess had gained influence in the local church, and was seducing the believers to commit sin. Jesus says those believers in Thyatira who do not repent will experience "great tribulation." The Greek word rendered "tribulation" occurs a number of times in Scripture in passages that have nothing to do with the tribulation period in the end time (e.g. Matt. 13:21; Rom. 5:3). In some places, it is translated "affliction" (e.g. 2 Cor. 8:2) or "trouble" (e.g. 2 Cor. 1:8). The Greek term translated "great tribulation" also occurs in Acts 7:11, where it is rendered "great trouble." The text reads, "Now a famine and *great trouble* came over all the land of Egypt and Canaan." This shows that the Greek term in question need not refer to the great tribulation in the end time.

It is apparent that the tribulation Jesus spoke of in Revelation 2:22 was a personal judgment on individuals in the church in Thyatira who allowed themselves to be seduced by the false prophetess, and would not repent. Therefore, they would experience much affliction. That Jesus is not saying that only spiritually adulterous believers will enter into the great tribulation is apparent because all believers are called to endure tribulation from the world (cf. Matt. 24:9; John 16:33; Acts 14:22; Rom. 8:35; 12:12). This also applies in the end time when tribulation will intensify and become "great tribulation" (Matt. 24:21; Rev. 7:14), which faithful followers of Christ will have to endure (cf. Rev. 13:10; 14:12).

"COME UP HERE"

"After these things I looked, and behold, a door standing open in heaven. And the first voice which I heard was like a trumpet speaking with me, saying, 'Come up here, and I will show you things which must take place after this.' Immediately I was in the Spirit; and behold, a throne set in heaven, and One sat on the throne." (Rev. 4:1, 2)

Doesn't John represent the church in that what happened to him is a picture of what will happen to the church? Doesn't this imply that the church will be transferred to heaven before the great tribulation?

There isn't anything in the passage to suggest that John is supposed to illustrate the church. We are only told that John was transported to heaven to see what will happen in the end time. In fact, John was not only in heaven when he received his visions. Later in the book of Revelation, he received several visions while on the earth (9:1–11; 10:1–5; 11:1; 13:1; 17:1–3; 18:1). If John really does portray the church, then this must mean the church will ascend to heaven and descend to the earth again a number of times during the great tribulation. This interpretation is, of course, unacceptable.

The first two verses in Revelation 4 are far too weak a foundation on which to build a theory of a transfer of the church to heaven before the great tribulation.

"SEVEN LAMPS OF FIRE"

In Revelation 4:5, we read, "And there were seven lamps of fire burning before the throne." Aren't the "seven lamps of fire" the same as "the seven lampstands" that Christ says are "the seven churches" (Rev. 1:20)? The seven lampstands that were on the earth are seen burning before the throne of God. Doesn't this mean the church will be transferred to heaven before the great tribulation?

The rest of Revelation 4:5 reads, "And there were seven lamps of fire burning before the throne, *which are the seven Spirits of God.*" It should be clear the church cannot be designated as "Spirits of God."

When John wrote to the seven churches, he greets them with grace and peace from God, Jesus Christ, and "the seven Spirits" (Rev. 1:4, 5). This suggests that "the seven Spirits" is a term that denotes the Holy Spirit. This can be certified by Isaiah 11:2, where the Holy Spirit is portrayed as seven Spirits: "The Spirit of the Lord [1], The Spirit of wisdom [2] and understanding [3], The Spirit of counsel [4] and might [5], The Spirit of knowledge [6] and of the fear of the Lord [7]." This passage describes seven characteristics of the Spirit of the Lord. In Revelation 3:1, we are told that Jesus "has the seven Spirits of God," i.e. He has the Holy Spirit who is "the Spirit of Christ" (1 Pet. 1:11).

We conclude from this that Revelation 4:5 does not show that the church will be in heaven during the great tribulation.

"THE SEVEN SPIRITS OF GOD"

In Revelation 4:5, we read about "the seven Spirits of God" that are "before the throne" in heaven. Don't they portray the Holy Spirit in heaven after having arrived there with the church before the great tribulation?

In the next chapter in the book of Revelation, we read about "the seven Spirits of God sent out into all the earth" (Rev. 5:6). This implies that even though the Holy Spirit is shown to be in heaven, He is simultaneously on the earth. In other words, He is omnipresent (Ps. 139:7–10).

The Bible shows that the Holy Spirit dwells in the believers (John 14:17), and since believers will evidently be on the earth during the great tribulation (e.g. Rev. 12:17; 14:12), He cannot possibly be confined to heaven at this time. The mention of repentance as a possibility in the great tribulation (Rev. 9:20, 21; 16:9) also shows that the Holy Spirit is present, because He is the One who makes repentance possible (John 16:7–11). Therefore, it cannot be said that the Holy Spirit is no longer operating on the earth the last years before Jesus returns.

We conclude that Revelation 4:5 gives no indication that the church will be transferred to heaven before the great tribulation.

"A SEA OF GLASS"

In Revelation 4:6, we read, "Before the throne there was a sea of glass, like crystal." Isn't the "sea of glass" a symbol of the church that will be transferred to heaven before the great tribulation?

We find another reference to the sea of glass later in the book of Revelation: "And I saw something like a sea of glass mingled with fire, and those who have the victory over the beast, over his image and over the number of his name, standing on the sea of glass, having harps of God" (15:2). Here, we see martyrs, who having overcome the Antichrist, stand on the sea of glass in heaven. This tells us the sea of glass cannot symbolize people, since people stand on it. We can therefore disregard the assertion that the sea of glass is a symbol of the church. This means Revelation 4:6 cannot be used to show that the church is in heaven during the great tribulation.

"AVENGE OUR BLOOD"

In Revelation 6:10, we read, "And they [the martyrs] cried with a loud voice, saying, 'How long, O Lord, holy and true, until You judge and avenge our blood on those who dwell on the earth?'" These martyrs cry to the Lord for revenge. They are very unlike Stephen, the first martyr of the church, who we read about in Acts 7:60: "Then he knelt down and cried out with a loud voice, 'Lord, do not charge them with this sin.'" Doesn't this mean the martyrs in Revelation 6 are a group of saved people from the great tribulation, while the church is in heaven?

The martyrs of the church have not all had, or will have, the same disposition as Stephen. Those in Revelation 6 were brutally "slain [literally: 'butchered'] for the testimony which they held" (v.9). Who can really blame them for longing for the Lord to "judge and avenge" their blood (v.10)? In fact, we are told that when Jesus returns He will take "vengeance on those" who "trouble" the believers (2 Thess. 2:6–8).

Notice the Lord does not reprimand the martyrs. We only read, "It was said to them that they should rest a little while longer, until both the number of their fellow servants and their brethren, who would be killed as they were, was completed" (v.11). This tells us the appointed number of martyrs will not be complete until the end of the great tribulation. Then the Lord will return and the resurrection of the dead in Christ will happen (1 Thess. 4:16), which includes the martyrs.

Based on the above observations, there is no reason to view these martyrs as a group of saved people who do not belong to the church. Hence, we cannot conclude from Revelation 6:10 that the church will be in heaven during the great tribulation.

"A GREAT MULTITUDE"

In Revelation 7:9, John sees "a great multitude which no one could number, of all nations, tribes, peoples, and tongues, standing before the throne and before the Lamb, clothed with white robes, with palm branches in their hands." In verse 14, John is told, "These are the ones who come out of the great tribulation, and washed their robes and made them white in the blood of the Lamb." Isn't the "great multitude" the church that will "come out of," i.e. escape the great tribulation by being transferred to heaven before this time comes?

This way of interpreting the phrase "come out of" is incorrect because of several reasons.

To begin with, in verse 13 one of the elders in heaven asks John about this great crowd: "Who are these arrayed in white robes, and *where* did they come from?" John answered, "Sir, you know." Then he is told, "These are the ones who come out of the great tribulation" (v.14). The answer to where they came from is the great tribulation. This means that they had been in the great tribulation, but now have come out of it.

In verse 16, it is said of the great crowd: "They shall neither hunger anymore nor thirst anymore," and in verse 17, we read, "And God will wipe away every tear from their eyes." This tells us of the trials they experienced on the earth (suffering hunger and thirst is usual during persecution). We cannot ignore that this may refer to certain trials in the great tribulation, when, for example, it won't be possible to buy food and drink without having "the mark or the name of the beast" (Rev. 13:17).

We read that the people in the great crowd are "clothed with white robes" (Rev. 7:9). They are dressed in the same way as the martyrs in Revelation 6:9 & 10. Concerning these, we are told: "Then each of them was given *a white robe*, and they were told to wait a *little* longer, until the number of their fellow servants and brothers who were to be killed as they had been was completed" (Rev. 6:11). It appears the great crowd in chapter 7 is comprised of the martyrs "fellow servants and brothers" who are slain in the *little* while of the great tribulation.

The text says the people in the great crowd "come out of the great tribulation." The Greek word rendered "come" denotes a present continuous action. This tells us those who make up the great crowd do not arrive in heaven all at the same time. As they are martyred, they "come out of the great tribulation" and their spirits are transported to heaven. At the end of the great tribulation, they appear as a great crowd as John saw.

The account of the "great multitude" seems to be an anticipatory parenthesis in the course of end time events shown to John. This vision comes early in the book of Revelation to show believers that God will recompense those who suffer martyrdom in the great tribulation.

"CAUGHT UP TO GOD"

In Revelation 12:5, we read, "And her Child was caught up to God and to His throne." Isn't the "Child" the church that will be transferred to heaven before the great tribulation?

At the beginning of verse 5, we read the following about the woman's son: "And she bore a male Child who was to *rule all nations with a rod of iron*." We find a reference to this in chapter 19: "Now out of His mouth goes a sharp sword, that with it He should strike *the nations*. And He Himself will *rule them with a rod of iron*" (v.15). The context clearly shows that Jesus is the one referred to here, not the church.

In the last part of Revelation 12:5, we read that the "Child was caught up to God and to *His throne*." That this can be said of Jesus is seen from His own words: "I . . . overcame and sat down with My Father on *His throne*" (Rev. 3:21). This happened after His resurrection when He was "taken up . . . into heaven" (Acts 1:11). Revelation 12:5 cannot therefore be used to show that the church will be transferred to heaven before the great tribulation.

"HIS TABERNACLE"

In Revelation 13:6, we read, "Then he opened his mouth in blasphemy against God, to blaspheme His name, His tabernacle, and those who dwell in heaven." Since Paul says the church is "a habitation of God" (Eph. 2:22), and the Antichrist blasphemes God's "tabernacle (i.e. His habitation) and those who dwell in heaven," doesn't this mean the church will be transferred to heaven before the time of the Antichrist?

The church is not the only entity that is called God's habitation in the Bible. Heaven itself is the habitation of God as we can see from these prayers: "Look down from Your holy *habitation*, from heaven" (Deut. 26:15), and: "Look down from heaven, and see from Your *habitation*, holy and glorious" (Is. 63:15).

In Revelation 15:5, we read of God's tabernacle that the Antichrist blasphemes in Revelation 13:6. There it says, "After this I looked and in heaven the temple, that is, the *tabernacle* of the Testimony, was opened." Obviously, this cannot be said of the church.

The Antichrist not only blasphemes God's name and His tabernacle; he also blasphemes "those who dwell in heaven." These are most probably cherubim, seraphim, the angels of heaven, and may include those who died as believers.

From this, I conclude that Revelation 13:6 is no proof that the church will be transferred to heaven before the Antichrist arises.

"WAR WITH THE SAINTS"

In Revelation 13:7, we read, "And it was granted him to make war with the saints and to overcome them." This is the same as Daniel 7:21, which speaks of the Antichrist "making war against the saints." Since Jesus says of the church in Matthew

16:18 that "the gates of Hades shall not prevail against it," doesn't this mean these saints are Jews, and not the church that will be taken to heaven before the great tribulation?

We can view Revelation 13:7, where it says the Antichrist will be granted *"to make war with the* saints," in the light of Revelation 12:17: "And the dragon . . . went *to make war with the* rest of her offspring, who *keep the commandments of God* and have *the testimony of Jesus Christ.*" Paul describes people in the church as those *"keeping the commandments of God"* (1 Cor. 7:19), and having *"the testimony of Christ"* (1 Cor. 1:6). This shows that those the Antichrist will "make war with" are people who belong to the church.

In regards to Daniel chapter 7, it should be noted that an angel tells here of people whom he calls "the saints of the Most High" (v.18). Daniel himself refers to these people as "the saints" in verse 21. In verse 27, the angel said, "The kingdoms under the whole heaven, shall be *given* to the people, *the saints* of the Most High." Jesus said to His disciples who became leaders in the church: "It is your Father's good pleasure to *give* you the kingdom" (Luke 12:32). Thus, "the saints" the angel told Daniel about who the Antichrist persecutes are those who make up the church, both Jew and Gentile who believe in Jesus Christ.

That "the saints" in Revelation 13:7 are people who believe in the Lord Jesus, is evident from Revelation 14:12, which reads, "Here is the patience of *the saints*; here are those who keep the commandments of God and the faith of Jesus." Thus, "the saints" in the book of Revelation are clearly believers. We should also note that Paul employed the expression "the saints" of believers who constitute the church (2 Cor. 1:1; Eph. 1:1; Phil. 1:1; Col. 1:2; etc.).

When Jesus spoke about "the gates of Hades" not prevailing against the church, He could not possibly have meant that believers would avoid suffering persecution by being imprisoned and martyred. From the very beginning of the church and throughout its history believers have suffered persecution by these means (cf. Acts 4:3; 5:18; 7:58; 8:1, 3; 12:1–4; 14:19; 16:22–24; 22:4; 24:27). The true church has always had to suffer for the sake of Christ's name, and many millions have become martyrs throughout the centuries. Concerning the present time, we only have to think about what befalls believers in Muslim countries, as well as communist states. Even so, the church is victorious despite persecution. The blood of the martyrs has always been the seed of the church.

The believers who lay down their lives in the great tribulation overcome Satan and the Antichrist—although in the natural, the opposite seems true. We read in Revelation 12:11: "And *they overcame him* [Satan] by the blood of the Lamb and by the word of their testimony, and they did not love their lives to the death." John wrote also the following about the martyrs from the great tribulation: "And I saw . . . those who have the *victory over the beast*, over his image and over his mark and over the number of his name, standing on the sea of glass" (Rev. 15:2).

From the above, we see there isn't anything in Revelation 13:7 to imply that the church will be taken to heaven before the great tribulation.

"ALL WHO DWELL ON THE EARTH"

"And all the world marveled and followed the beast. . . . And authority was given him over every tribe, tongue, and nation. And all who dwell on the earth will worship him. . . . He was granted power to . . . cause as many as would not worship the image of the beast to be killed." (Rev. 13:3, 7, 8, 15)

Since everyone in the world either will worship the Antichrist or be killed, doesn't this mean the church must be fetched to heaven before he rises to power?

According to Jesus, there will be righteous individuals who survive the tribulation period and enter the kingdom after His judgment of all the nations at His return (Matt. 25:31–46). This implies there will be people who neither worship the Antichrist, nor are killed. The Antichrist will intend to kill all those who do not submit to him, but he will not be successful. One reason for this is that he will only have three and a half years to wage war on the saints (Rev. 13:5, 7).

Scripture indicates there will be believers who are still alive at the end of the great tribulation when Jesus returns. Paul alludes to surviving believers when he writes of the coming of Jesus and the resurrection of the dead: "*We who are still alive and are left* [lit. 'survive'] will be caught up together with them in the clouds to meet the Lord in the air" (1 Thess. 4:17).

Therefore, the consequence of refusing to worship the Antichrist does not mean the church has to be fetched to heaven before he rises to power.

"KEEP THE COMMANDMENTS OF GOD"

In Revelation 14:12, we read about "the saints . . . who keep the commandments of God and the faith of Jesus." Aren't these Jewish believers in the great tribulation since they "keep the commandments of God"? Doesn't this mean the church will be transferred to heaven before the great tribulation?

The saints in Revelation 14 are mentioned in chapter 12 as those "who keep *the commandments of God* and have *the testimony* of Jesus Christ" (v.17). Saints who become martyrs are portrayed in chapter 6 as "those who had been slain for *the word of God* and for *the testimony* which they held" (v.9). The apostle John says of himself that he "was on the island that is called Patmos for *the word of God* and for *the testimony* of Jesus Christ" (1:9). In these three references, we see that the expression "the commandments of God" is equivalent to "the word of God," both of which are connected to "the testimony" of Jesus Christ.

The same John, who wrote the book of Revelation, wrote also about "the testimony" in 1 John 5:10 & 11, and about keeping the commandments of God (1 John 2:3, 4, 7, 8; 3:22-24; 4:21; 5:2, 3). He says that keeping the commandments of God is the same as keeping the word of God. In 1 John 2:4, he writes, "keep His commandments" and in the very next verse, "keeps His word." This was of course written to all believers, and can be compared to Christ's message to the church in Philadelphia: "You have . . . kept My word" (Rev. 3:8). It should therefore be evident that the saints who "keep the commandments of God and the faith of Jesus" in Revelation 14 cannot be limited to believing Jews, but comprise all believers. The church, which consists of both believing Jews and Gentiles (Eph. 2:11-19), is therefore portrayed as being present in the great tribulation.

The Scriptures do not give any indication of a division between believers, where some are taken out of the world before the great tribulation, while others are present at that time. On the contrary, we read that Jesus said, "I am with you always, even to the end of the age" (Matt. 28:20). What Jesus called "the end of the age" will come when He returns after the great tribulation (cf. Matt. 24:3, 21, 29-31). Jesus was speaking of His spiritual presence with all those who belong to Him until He physically returns to the earth.

In connection with the end time, Paul tells us the following: "Hardening in part has happened to Israel until the fullness of the Gentiles has come in. And so all Israel will be saved, as it is written: The Deliverer will come out of Zion, and He will turn away ungodliness from Jacob" (Rom. 11:25, 26). Here, we see that the church will not be complete until all the surviving Jews are saved at the coming of "the Deliverer" (Christ), which happens after the great tribulation. As with Jesus, Paul does not make any division between the church and believers in the great tribulation.

Based on the above, Revelation 14:12 cannot be used to imply that the church will be in heaven during the great tribulation.

"THE BOWLS OF THE WRATH OF GOD"

We read in Revelation 16 about "the bowls of the wrath of God" being poured out. Since God will not allow the believers to be overtaken by His wrath, doesn't this mean the church will be transferred to heaven before the great tribulation?

By taking a closer look at the effects of the bowls of wrath in Revelation 16, we find they do not target the believers on the earth. We are told God's wrath is directed toward those "who had the mark of the beast and those who worshiped his image" (v.2). This is in line with what we read in chapter 14, where it says, "If anyone worships the beast and his image, and receives his mark on his forehead or on his hand, he himself shall drink of the wine of the wrath of God, which is poured out full strength into the cup of His indignation" (vv.9, 10).

The seven bowls of the wrath of God, also called "the seven plagues" (15:8), are similar to some of the plagues and judgments that struck Egypt when the people of Israel came out of bondage. The following is a comparison of the two:

Bowls of Wrath (Rev. 16)	Judgments of God (Exodus)
1) "A foul and loathsome *sore* came upon the men who had the mark of the beast." (v.2)	"[The ashes] caused boils that break out in *sores* on man and beast." (9:10)
2) "Every living creature in the sea *died*." (v.3)	"The fish that were in the river *died*." (7:21)
3) "The *rivers* and springs of water . . . became *blood*." (v.4)	"All the *waters* in the *river* were turned to *blood*." (7:20)

4) "Power was given to him   "*Fire* darted to
   to scorch men with *fire*." (v.8)   the ground." (9:23)

5) "The beast['s] . . . kingdom   "There was thick *darkness*
   became full of *darkness*." (v.10) in all the land." (10:22)

6) "The great river Euphrates   "The Lord . . . made the
   . . . was *dried* up." (v.12)   sea into *dry* land." (14:21)

7) "Great *hail* from heaven fell   "The *hail* struck . . . both
   upon men, every hailstone about   man and beast . . . and broke
   the weight of a talent." (v.21)   every tree of the field." (9:25)

When the judgments of God struck Egypt, a difference was made between the people of Israel and the Egyptians. For example, we read, "All the livestock of Egypt died; but of the livestock of the children of Israel, not one died" (Ex. 9:6). Concerning the hail, we read, "Only in the land of Goshen, where the children of Israel were, there was no hail" (v.26). In connection with the darkness that came over Egypt, we are told the following: "They did not see one another; nor did anyone rise from his place for three days. But all the children of Israel had light in their dwellings" (Ex. 10:23). When the Lord struck all the firstborn in Egypt, the Israelites were spared when He saw lamb's blood on the entrances of their homes (Ex. 12:23). All these plagues struck the Egyptians, but the Israelites were safe because they were under the protective hand of God.

At the end of the great tribulation, these judgments are going to be repeated, but this time on a much larger scale. In the same way as the people of Israel were not the recipients of the judgments, the believers are going to be protected from the effects of the bowls of wrath. It will be as the Lord said to Pharaoh through Moses: "I will make a difference between My people and your people" (Ex. 8:23).

In connection with the seventh bowl, we read, "And great Babylon was remembered before God, to give her the cup of the wine of the fierceness of His wrath" (Rev. 16:19). We are told the believers will be spared if they obey God: "And I heard another voice from heaven saying, 'Come out of her, My people, lest you share in her sins, and lest you receive of her plagues'" (Rev. 18:4). The wrath of God will not befall the believers who come out of "Babylon." However, it will overtake the ungodly, as also Paul says: "For the wrath of God is revealed from heaven against all ungodliness and unrighteousness of men, who suppress the truth in unrighteousness" (Rom. 1:18).

Between the sixth and seventh bowl, Jesus says: "Behold, I am coming as a thief. Blessed is he who watches" (Rev. 16:15). This is an announcement to the believers that the coming of Christ will then be very near. Here, we see another indication that the believers are on the earth at the time of the bowls.

Since the believers on the earth will not be affected by the wrath of God, this means they do not have to be transferred to heaven before the bowls of wrath are poured out.

"THE MARRIAGE OF THE LAMB"

In Revelation 19:7, we read, "The marriage of the Lamb has come, and His wife has made herself ready." Verse 9 says, "Blessed are those who are called to the marriage supper of the Lamb!" Since the marriage will take place in heaven before Christ returns to the earth, doesn't this mean the church will be transferred to heaven before the great tribulation?

Revelation 19 begins with praise to God for the destruction of Babylon. In this connection, there are four shouts of "Hallelujah" (vv.1, 3, 4, 6). It is only after this that we hear about "the marriage of the Lamb" (v.7). Thus, the "marriage" is spoken of *after* the destruction of Babylon, which is among the last things to happen in the great tribulation before Jesus returns to the earth. At the outpouring of the seventh bowl, Revelation 16:19 says, "God remembered Babylon the Great and gave her the cup filled with the wine of the fury of His wrath." Then follow chapters 17 and 18, which describe Babylon and its destruction.

The utterances about "the marriage of the Lamb" in Revelation 19 sound as in anticipation of something that is going to happen. They are an announcement of the forthcoming wedding celebration, but the actual event is not described. Immediately after the announcement, we see Christ on a white horse coming down from heaven to defeat the Antichrist (v.11 ff). This indicates "the marriage of the Lamb" will take place when Christ returns after the great tribulation; it will not happen in heaven during the tribulation period.

In connection with His return and the coming kingdom, Jesus said:

> There will be weeping and gnashing of teeth, when you see Abraham and Isaac and Jacob and all the prophets in the kingdom of God, and you yourselves thrust out. They will come from the east and the west, from the north and the south, and *sit down* in the kingdom of God. (Luke 13:28, 29)

The expression "sit down" here seems to point to "the marriage supper of the Lamb" since Jesus tells in the next chapter of those who "sit down" at "a wedding feast" (14:7–11). The "marriage supper of the Lamb" seems therefore to be held on the earth when Jesus has come and set up the future kingdom.

In one of His parables, Jesus said the future kingdom of God is "like a certain king who arranged a marriage for his son" (Matt. 22:2). Jesus also told about "those who were invited to the wedding" (Matt. 22:3). This can be compared to Revelation 19:9 that mentions "those who are called [i.e. invited] to the marriage supper of the Lamb." What Jesus spoke of can be connected to what He said to His disciples at the inauguration of the Communion: "I will not drink of this fruit of the vine from now on until that day when I drink it new with you *in My Father's kingdom*" (Matt. 26:29). Here, we see that Jesus will again drink wine only when the kingdom has come—this time to celebrate His "marriage." This is another indication that "the marriage of the Lamb" will take place when Jesus has returned and set up the kingdom on the earth.

The identity of the bride is yet another indication that "the marriage of the Lamb" will take place after the great tribulation, and not in heaven while the great tribulation is in progress on the earth. We read about the bride of Christ in Revelation 19:8: "And to her it was granted to be arrayed in fine linen, clean and bright, for the fine linen is the righteous acts of *the saints*." This tells us the bride is made up of "the saints." These saints are mentioned earlier in the book of Revelation, e.g., "And it was granted to him [the Antichrist] to make war with *the saints*" (Rev. 13:7), and, "Here is the patience and the faith of *the saints*" (Rev. 13:10). It is plain to see that the saints, i.e. the bride, are present in the great tribulation when the Antichrist reigns.

At the end of the great tribulation, it will be said of Christ's saints, "His wife has made herself ready" (Rev. 19:7). Jesus will then come and the resurrection and rapture of the believers will occur (1 Thess. 4:16, 17). They will be clothed in "fine linen, clean and bright" (Rev. 19:8), and meet the Groom in the air. Then "the marriage of the Lamb" will be celebrated in the kingdom of God, which at this time will be set up on the earth. This event will mark the beginning of the eternal union between Jesus and the church, as the last part of 1 Thessalonians 4:17 says: "And thus we shall always be with the Lord."

As to the location of the marriage supper, a prophecy in the book of Isaiah provides the answer. In the last verse of chapter 24, we read of the end time cosmic signs after the great tribulation (cf. Matt. 24:29) followed by Christ's coming to reign on the earth: "The moon will be disgraced and the sun ashamed; for the Lord of hosts will reign on *Mount Zion* and in Jerusalem" (Is. 24:23). A few verses later a description of the marriage supper is given: "The Lord of hosts will prepare a lavish banquet for all peoples on *this mountain* [Mount Zion]; a banquet of aged wine, choice pieces with marrow" (Is. 25:6).

Thus, the marriage supper will be held on Mount Zion in Jerusalem when Jesus has returned. This means that the statements in Revelation 19 concerning the marriage of the Lamb do not require the church to be fetched to heaven before the great tribulation.

"THE ARMIES IN HEAVEN"

In Revelation 19:11, it says: "Then I saw heaven opened, and behold, a white horse. And He who sat on him was called Faithful and True, and in righteousness He judges and makes war." This verse and the remainder of the chapter describe the return of Christ to the earth after the great tribulation. In verse 14, we read of "the armies in heaven, clothed in fine linen, white and clean" that follow Christ. Since verse 8 says of the bride of Christ, "And to her it was granted to be arrayed in fine linen, clean and bright," doesn't this mean the armies are the believers following Christ from heaven, where they were transferred to before the great tribulation?

There is much evidence to show that the "armies in heaven" who accompany Jesus are, in fact, armies of angels. Jesus said about His return: "When the Son of Man comes in His glory, and all the holy angels with Him" (Matt. 25:31). Thus, we would expect to see all the angels accompany Jesus at His second coming that is portrayed in Revelation 19.

According to Jesus, the angels are organized into armies. He once said that He could have prayed to His Father to send Him "more than twelve legions of angels" (Matt. 26:53). The term legion" refers to about six thousand soldiers. In Revelation 12, we see the angelic army in battle. Verse 7 says, "Michael and his angels fought with the dragon; and the dragon and his angels fought."

The armies that accompany Jesus ride "on white horses" (Rev. 19:14). That they are angels is supported by the account in 2 Kings 6. In verse 17, the prophet Elisha prayed that God would open the eyes of his servant, and he saw the mountain "full of *horses* and chariots of fire." These heavenly horses certainly belong to the "armies in heaven."

As to the clothing of the heavenly armies ("fine linen, white and clean"), we read in Revelation 15:6 about "angels . . . clothed in pure bright linen." Also John 20:12 tells us of "angels in white." The heavenly armies who accompany Jesus in His descent to the earth are undoubtedly the angels of heaven. To insist that the "armies in heaven" are the bride of Christ from their similar clothing is insufficient evidence; Jesus infers to this similarity in Mark 12:25, where He says those who are resurrected "are like angels." This coming resurrection of the believers is alluded to in Revelation 19:8: "And to her [the bride of Christ] it was granted to be arrayed in fine linen, clean and bright." The timing of this change of clothing appears to be when Jesus is revealed from heaven coming on a white horse (v.11 ff). The bride receives her new apparel when she is clothed with imperishableness and immortality in the resurrection at the time of the rapture to meet her Bridegroom. Paul says:

> We will all be changed—in a flash, in the twinkling of an eye, at the last trumpet. For the trumpet will sound, the dead will be raised imperishable, and we will be changed. For the perishable must *clothe* itself with the imperishable, and the mortal with immortality. (1 Cor. 15:51–53)

Having met Jesus in the air at the rapture (1 Thess. 4:17), the believers will partake in His victory over the Antichrist when He continues His descent to the earth with them and the angels. Revelation 17:14 says, "The Lamb will overcome them [the Antichrist and the ten kings], for He is Lord of lords and King of kings; and *those who are with Him* are called, chosen, and faithful."

That the catching up of the believers to the clouds is not directly mentioned in the description of Christ's return in Revelation 19 can be due to this passage being primarily concerned with Christ's victory over "the beast, the kings of the earth, and their armies" (v.19). John gives just a short description of Christ's take-over of the world when He comes. Nothing is said of the glory Jesus is going to come with, nor of the clouds

He will come in, nor of the Jewish remnant He will save when He comes. At the same time, John gives us details that are not mentioned by others who wrote about the return of Christ in the Bible; e.g. that Jesus rides on a white horse, as well as a description of His clothing (vv.12, 13, 16). Other writers give us more knowledge of the events that will occur when Jesus returns; e.g. only the prophet Zechariah informs us that Jesus will descend on the Mount of Olives (Zech. 14:4), and only Paul tells us that the gathering of the resurrected and glorified believers when Jesus returns will happen in the air (1 Thess. 4:16, 17). Paul, John, Zechariah and the other prophets and apostles wrote and spoke prophetically in part only. The complete picture is formed when we put all the pieces together.

According to what we have looked at, the verses in question from Revelation 19 cannot be used to show that the church will be transferred to heaven before the great tribulation.

"THEY LIVED AND REIGNED"

"And I saw thrones, and they sat on them, and judgment was committed to them. And I saw the souls of those who had been beheaded for their witness to Jesus and for the word of God, who had not worshiped the beast or his image, and had not received his mark on their foreheads or on their hands. And they lived and reigned with Christ for a thousand years." (Rev. 20:4)

Isn't this is a description of the resurrection of the martyrs from the great tribulation after Christ returns to the earth, and therefore separate from the resurrection of believers that occurs before the great tribulation?

By taking a closer look at this verse, we see two groups. The first group is in the first part of the verse: "And I saw thrones, and they sat on them, and judgment was committed to them."

Sitting on thrones and judging in Christ's kingdom is in accordance with promises that are given to all believers earlier in the book of Revelation (2:26; 3:21; 5:10). This aligns with Paul's statement that "the saints (the believers) will [one day] judge and govern the world" (1 Cor. 6:2 AMP). This suggests that the first part of Revelation 20:4 portrays believers reigning with Christ.

The second group consists of martyrs from the great tribulation. They are singled out for special attention in the last part of the verse: "And I saw the souls of those who had been beheaded for their witness to Jesus and for the word of God who had not worshiped the beast or his image, and had not received his mark on their foreheads or on their hands. And they lived and reigned with Christ for a thousand years."

The next verse says, "This is the first resurrection." Since this resurrection concerns, among others, the martyrs from the great tribulation, this tells us that a resurrection of millions of believers cannot have take place several years earlier, i.e. prior to the great tribulation. If such a resurrection were to take place then what is portrayed in verse 4 would be a second resurrection, which it obviously is not. There will be a second resurrection, but this concerns "the rest of the dead" when "the thousand years were finished" (v.5). This means the first resurrection involves all believers, including the martyrs. The resurrection of the martyrs is therefore not separate from the resurrection of the other believers.

According to Jesus, the resurrection of all the believers will happen on "the last day." He said, "Everyone who sees the Son and believes in Him may have everlasting life; and I will raise him up at the last day" (John 6:40). The "last day" comes at the very end of the age, i.e. after the great tribulation.

When conducting a word study of Revelation 20:4, we find that John did not actually witness the resurrection of the dead, only the aftermath. The Greek word rendered "lived" in the excerpt "they lived and reigned" does not mean the actual act of being raised from the dead. The word is *ezesan*, and is also used in Revelation 2:8, where Jesus said that He "was dead and is *alive*." It conveys the state of being alive, in this case after having been raised from the dead. The meaning of what John wrote can be formulated in this way: 'They were living (after having been raised) and reigned.' This shows the resurrection had already occurred when John saw those sitting on thrones. In other words, we are not to presume the resurrection occurs in chapter 20. The resurrection will happen when Christ returns after the great tribulation in chapter 19. Paul is in line with this when he wrote of the raising of "the dead in Christ" when Christ returns (1 Thess. 4:16).

We conclude that what John observed in Revelation 20:4 are the resurrected believers as co-regents with Jesus in the kingdom that will be set up on the earth when He returns. Special attention is given to those believers who become martyrs during the great tribulation. Thus, this verse cannot be used to infer that there will be a resurrection of believers before the great tribulation.

"THE BRIGHT AND MORNING STAR"

Isn't Christ going to come before the great tribulation as the morning star (Rev. 22:16) when He will be seen only by the believers, and then after the great tribulation as the sun (Mal. 4:2) to be seen by the entire world?

By looking at the verse in question from the book of Revelation, we do not find that Jesus is going to come as the morning star. We only read that Jesus says of Himself, "I am the Root and Offspring of David, the Bright and Morning Star." This may allude to the messianic prophecy in Numbers 24:17: "A Star shall come out of Jacob."

Jesus has many names and titles in the Bible. However, it is mere speculation to use one of them to assert that Jesus will come unseen by the world before the great tribulation.

"I AM COMING SOON"

Since Jesus said, "I am coming soon" (Rev. 22:20), doesn't this mean that no prophetic event needs to happen before He comes?

The word rendered "soon" in this verse is the Greek word *tachu*. Besides carrying the meaning of "shortly," it also means "quickly" as several other translations render it. Whatever way this word is translated, we need to be aware that what the Lord says in Revelation 22:20 must be reckoned from His viewpoint, not ours. The apostle Peter wrote: "But, beloved, do not forget this one thing, that with the Lord one day is as a thousand years, and a thousand years as one day. The Lord is not slack concerning His promise [of His coming – v.4], as some count slackness" (2 Pet. 3:8, 9).

This tells us that from the time Jesus uttered the promise of His coming to the apostle John in Revelation 22, only a couple of days have passed from the Lord's perspective. The fact that two thousand years have now passed bears out that when Jesus said He is coming "soon" (or quickly) He did not mean that no prophetic event needs to happen before He comes. Among the things Jesus said would transpire before He can return, is that "the gospel must first be preached to all the nations" (Mark 13:10; cf. Rev. 14:6, 7). Only then will Jesus come back, as described in Revelation 19:11 ff.

A Final Word

In this exhaustive study we have examined what the Bible says about the return of Christ in relation to the coming time of great tribulation. We have seen that the Scriptures of the Old Testament do not show that Jesus will come back before the great tribulation. In the Gospels, we see that Jesus taught He would come back after the great tribulation, gather those who belong to Him, and reign on the earth. In the letters of the New Testament, we see that Paul and other apostles depict the same scenario. Also in the Book of Revelation, we see the same picture presented. The teaching of the entire Bible concerning the end time and the second coming of Jesus is therefore coherent and unified.

The idea that believers are going to be transferred to heaven before the time of great tribulation is attractive and easy to embrace. However, based on our study this theory does not have a solid anchorage in the teaching of Jesus and the apostles. We have seen that the rapture of the believers to the clouds and the return of Christ to the earth will happen in close succession after the period of great tribulation in the end time. The gathering of all the believers in the clouds to meet Jesus will happen as He is descending to Jerusalem to reign on the earth together with all those who belong to Him.

Whether the time remaining until the return of Christ is long or short, a healthy attitude would be to prepare mentally, emotionally, and physically for hardship in the end time. By staying prayerfully in the Word of God we will be able to keep ourselves spiritually awake and not be deceived. Finally, maintaining a close walk with Jesus and serving Him faithfully will enable us to be ready for His return.

ABOUT THE AUTHOR

Robert Ivor Adams was born and raised in Britain in a Christian home. At the age of twelve, he received the Lord Jesus into his life, and developed a hunger to know the Word of God. As a teenager, he moved to Norway with the rest of his family. He has attended various Bible colleges, and has ministered in Norway and Pakistan—in churches, Bible schools, and house groups. Robert currently lives in southern Norway. He has a YouTube channel dedicated to the End Time called 'Last Days Detective,' where he has posted numerous teaching videos.

Visit also the author's website: www.lastdaysdetective.com

Another book by Robert I. Adams:

THE UNVEILING – A Guide to The Prophecies of The Book of Revelation

The world is heading toward a climax. End time prophecies in the book of Revelation are nearing the time of their fulfillment. As we get closer, it is imperative we understand what to expect will occur on the world scene.

Here are some questions about the last book of the Bible that we need answers to:

- What does it say about the future of the world?
- Where does it place the church in the last days?
- What does it say about Israel in the end time?
- How does it portray the return of Christ?

Robert I. Adams conveys with clarity and conviction what the book of Revelation reveals concerning these issues.

THE UNVEILING is available from lulu.com & amazon.com

Bibliography

ALEXANDER, J. C.: *The Kingdom of The Beast and The End of The World*, ACW Press 2005.

ALLEN, Stuart: *World Conditions and The End of The Age*, 1977.

ALTAF, Simon: *Islam Peace or Beast?* Your Arms To Yisrael Publishing, 2006.

AMES, Richard F.: *The Middle East In Prophecy*, Living Church of God, 2006.

ANDERSON, Sir Robert: *Forgotten Truths*, Kregel Publications 1980.

_____ . *The Coming Prince*, Kregel Publications 1984.

BARCLAY, William: *The Daily Study Bible*, The Saint Andrew Press - Scotland 1989–90.

BEASLEY-MURRAY, George R.: *Jesus and The Last Days,* Hendrickson Publishers 1993.

BERNIS, Jonathan: *A Rabbi Looks at the Last Days*, JVMI Publishing 2008.

BERRY, George Ricker: *Interlinear Greek-English New Testament*, Baker book House 1897/1987.

BETZER, Dan: *Countdown – A Newsman Looks at The Rapture*, Gospel Publishing House

BLAISING, Craig A.: *Dispensationalism, Israel and the Church*, Zondervan Publishing House 1992.

BLOOMFIELD, Arthur E.: *All Things New*, 1959.

_____ . *Before The Last Battle – Armageddon*, Bethany 1971.

_____ . *The End of The Days*, Bethany Fellowship 1961.

BULLINGER, Ethelbert W.: *Commentary On Revelation*, Kregel Publications 1984.

DAKE, Finis J.: *The Rapture and the Second Coming of Christ*, Dake Bible Sales 1977.

DEAL, Colin H.: *The Beast and The Arabs*, End Time Ministry. 1983.

_____. *The Day and Hour Jesus Will Return*, End Time Ministry 1981.

_____. *The Great Tribulation – How Long?* End Time Ministry 1991.

_____. *Will Christ Return By 1988?* End Time Ministry 1979.

DYER, Charles H.: *World News and Bible Prophecy*, Tyndale House 1993.

FOULKES, Francis: *Pocket Guide to The New Testament*, Inter-Varsity Press 1978.

GRAHAM, Dr. Billy: *Storm Warning*, Word Inc., 1992.

HAGEE, John: *Beginning of the End*, 1996.

HARRIS, Charles: *What's Ahead? – A Study of End time Events*, Gospel Publishing House 1981.

HICKS, Dr. Roy: *Another Look At The Rapture*, Harrison House 1982.

HINDSON, Ed: *End Times, The Middle East & The New World Order*, SP Publications, Inc., 1991.

HOEKEMA, Anthony A.: *The Bible and The Future*, WM. B. Eerdmans / The Paternoster Press 1979.

ICE, Thomas; Price, Randall: *Ready to Rebuild*, Harvest House Publishers 1993.

IRONSIDE, H.A.: *Not Wrath But Rapture*, Eagle books 1936.

JAMES, Edgar C.: *Day of The Lamb*, 1980.

JAMES, William T. (and others): *Earth's Final Days*, New Leaf Press 1995.

JOHSTON, Jerry: *The Last Days of Planet Earth*, Harvest House 1991.

LADD, George Eldon: *A Commentary on The Revelation of John*, Wm. B. Eerdmans 1972.

_____. *A Theology of The New Testament*, Wm. B. Eerdmans 1974.

_____. *The Blessed Hope*, Wm. B. Eerdmans 1956.

LAHAYE, Tim (& Jerry B. Jenkins): *Are We Living in the End Times?* Alive Communications, Inc. 1999.

_____. *Left behind* series, Tyndale House from 1995.

LALONDE, Peter & Paul: *The Mark of The Beast,* Harvest House Publishers 1994.

LARKIN, Clarence: *The Second Coming of Christ*, Rev. Clarence Larkin Estate 1918.

Life Application Bible, Kingsway Publications 1992.

LINDSEY, Hal: *The Late Great Planet Earth*, Zondervan 1970.

_____. *There's A New World Coming*, Coverdale House 1973.

LIVINGSTON, Robert: *Christianity and Islam: The Final Clash*, Pleasant Word 2004.

McCULLUM, Brian K.: *The Day of the Lord*, Rema Bible Church 1985.

McHYDE, Timothy J.: *Know the Future*, www.EscapeAllTheseThings.com 2003.

MEIER, Dr.Paul: *The Third Millenium*, Thomas Nelson Inc. 1997.

MILNE, Bruce: *Know The Truth*, Inter-Varsity Press 1982.

MORRIS, Leon: *1 and 2 Thessalonians*, Inter-Varsity Press/Wm. B. Eerdmans 1984.

_____. *Revelation*, Inter-Varsity Press/Wm. B. Eerdmans 1984.

NOÉ, John: *The Apocalypse Conspiracy*, Wolgemuth & Hyatt 1991.

PAWSON, David: *When Jesus Returns*, Hodder & Stoughton 1995.

PENTECOST, J. Dwight: *Things to Come*, Zondervan Publishing House 1958.

PIERCE & WASHABAUGH: *The Interpreters Bible*, Parthenon Press 1955-57.

RICHARDSON, Joel: *Antichrist Islam's Awaited Messiah*, Pleasant Word 2006.

SHOEBAT, Walid: *God's War on Terror*, Top Executive Media 2008.

SKOLFIELD, Ellis: *Islam In The End Times*, Fish House Ministries 2007.

SMITH, Chuck: *Snatched Away,* Maranatha Evangelical Association 1979.

SNYDER, Michael T.: *The Rapture Verdict*, Michael T. Snyder 2016.

Spirit-Filled Life Bible, Thomas Nelson Publishers 1991.

STEINLE, C. W.: *Why Most Christians Believe in Post-Tribulation Rapture*, C. W. Steinle 2016.

STICE, Ralph W.: *From 9/11 to 666*, ACW Press 2005.

SUMRALL, Lester: *I Predict 2000 A.D.*, LeSEA Publishing Company 1987.

SUTTON, Dr. Hilton: *Rapture – Get Right or Get Left*, Harrison House 1983.

TASKER, R.V.G.: *Matthew – An Introduction and Commentary*, The Tyndale Press 1961.

UNGER, Merrill F.: *The Hodder Bible Handbook*, Hodder & Stoughton 1984.

VAN IMPE, Dr. Jack: *Signs of The Times I*, Jack Van Impe Crusades 1976.

_____. *Signs of The Times II*, Jack Van Impe Crusades 1976.

_____. *What In The World Is Happening?* Jack Van Impe Crusades

1976.

WALVOORD, John F.: *The Rapture Question*, Dunham 1957.

_____. *Armageddon, Oil & The Middle East Crisis*, The Zondervan Corporation 1990.

_____. *Major Bible Prophecies*, Zondervan Publishing House 1991.

WANAMAKER, Charles A.: *Commentary On 1 & 2 Thessalonians*, WM. B. Eerdmans 1990.

WEBBER, Dr. David: *Is The Antichrist In The World Today?* Southwest Radio Church 1982.

WITHERINGTON III, Ben: *Jesus, Paul and The End of The World,* The Paternoster Press 1992.

YANDIAN, Bob: *Resurrection – Our Victory Over Death*, Harrison House 1986.

YONNGI Cho, David: *Revelation*, Creation House 1992.

ZODHIATES Th.D., Spiros: *Hebrew Greek Key Study Bible*, AMG Publications 1984.

Printed in Great Britain
by Amazon